BARRON'S

PAINLESS

Spelling

Mary Elizabeth, M.Ed.

Third Edition

All inquiries should be addressed to:
Barron's Educational Series, Inc.
250 Wireless Boulevard
Hauppauge, New York 11788
www.barronseduc.com

Library of Congress Catalog Card No.: 2010941464

ISBN: 978-0-7641-4713-5

PRINTED IN CANADA
9 8 7 6 5 4 3 2 1

This book is for Fr. Paa Kwesi Maison
and everyone—
born in the United States or elsewhere—
who tries to make sense of
English spelling

Acknowledgments

Thank you to the authors of *Words Their Way: Word Study for Phonics, Vocabulary, and Spelling Instruction,* whose intelligent and insightful developmental approach to spelling provided the categories around which I initially organized this book. Additional thanks go to Amy O'Meara for reviewing the new chapter, *Spelling in the 21st Century.*

CONTENTS

INTRODUCTION

Why learning to spell is important

Which is correct: *cosily* or *cozily? theater* or *theatre? analyze* or *analyse?* The answer may surprise you: they are ALL correct. And that's the first problem with spelling in English—sometimes there's more than one correct and standard way to write a word.

This has happened because:

- in some cases, the spelling of a word has changed over time;
- U.S. and British spelling have become differentiated;
- altered spellings used for special purposes have become more acceptable;
- words from other languages have entered English, sometimes through multiple avenues, resulting in multiple spellings.

But that's only the beginning. Teeming with words borrowed from other languages, English can seem like an impossible language to spell correctly. Not to worry. This book will take you on a tour of *American English*—the name for the dialect of English spoken in the United States—and help you nail down the basics that will make spelling most English words less of a challenge.

Sure, you'll still run across words that are exceptions to the rules you learn. Because any word in a U.S. English dictionary, no matter what its origin, is considered English, at least occasionally, we have to work with spelling rules from many different languages of origin. For example, if you want to spell *qiviut*, the Inuit word for the undercoat of the musk ox, you have to ignore the general English rule that *q* is always followed by *u*. But remember that these are

Qiviut!

exceptions. For the most part, the guidelines in this book will help you steer cleanly through the inconsistencies in the strange and wonderful language we call English.

The second problem is that some people have gotten the mistaken idea that spelling is not very important in the 21st century. They argue that since most people do most of their writing on a computer, and using the spell checker is a cinch, we don't need to focus on spelling. Don't get taken in by this reasoning! If you type *through* instead of *threw*, or *their* instead of *there*, or *even* instead of *event*, your spell checker can't tell that you made a mistake—all six are perfectly good and correctly spelled English words. One study found that as many as 40 percent of spelling errors are real-word errors in which one word is mistakenly typed for another.

In addition, if you type *eggzasparated* instead of *exasperated*, your spell checker may not have a clue about what word you MEANT to type (mine didn't!). And if you're taking a pencil-and-paper exam, you won't get a chance to spell check your writing. Your teacher will judge you on your spelling, among other things. So you'll want to be prepared with a good, broad knowledge of how to spell English words.

The fact is, no matter how much technology you have to help you, you still need to know fundamental spelling rules in order to communicate with people. And that's the whole point! We don't learn spelling rules for the sake of learning the rules. The goal is to express ourselves in a way that others can understand. THAT'S the reason to learn more about spelling.

So we begin by setting the stage in Chapter 1, discussing the particular challenges of spelling in the 21st century. Why is this special or different? For one thing, we now interact far more with people who speak different dialects of English than we do. Another important point is that with the advent of text messaging and Twitter, the need to adapt to very short message lengths means that being good at shortened spellings is not only acceptable but also desirable. The result is two systems—the standard system and a shortened system—and with this alternative system comes the need to make decisions about when to use each one.

In Chapter 2, we begin by talking about visual and sound patterns in U.S. English, not only the frequent and obvious ones, but all of them. Some people would rather not know about the complications. And some spelling books don't give you a choice—in effect, they conceal the difficulties and focus only on the main spellings for each sound. My approach is different. I present a map for the whole territory, helping you to gain an overview of U.S. English spelling in this chapter, and then—like other spelling texts—start Chapter 3 with the basics and follow a progression from simpler to more complex spelling topics. If you want to put sticky notes on the chart pages and refer back to them, you can. If you don't want to, you don't have to. But they are there for your reference whenever you might need them.

Brain Tickler exercises will help you understand the relationships between spoken and written English and become more aware of the structure of written words and the relationships between words that are related. These exercises will also help you become more familiar with the characteristic patterns of the spelling of U.S. English. You can jot down your answers to the exercises on loose-leaf paper or in a notebook. By the time we're finished, you'll be able to spend more time thinking about what you're communicating instead of how to spell it correctly. And that's where it's at!

The dictionary we'll be using as our point of reference, unless otherwise noted, is *The American Heritage Dictionary of the English Language*, *4th ed.*

How English spelling was shaped by history

Do you know what a mongrel is? Sometimes we use the word *mongrel* to refer to a dog with a mixed background. So you can think of it as meaning "a mixture." The English language is a mongrel in this sense.

The English language came into being around A.D. 450. Three tribes from Northern Europe—the Angles, the Saxons, and the Jutes—invaded the British Isles. The main island came to be known as jolly old "Angle"land (England), and the language that came into being became known as Anglo-Saxon or **Old English**. Every one of the top 100 most frequently used words in English today comes from Old English.

I believe we are inventing a new language.

BRAIN TICKLERS
Set #1 English and Old English

Hey, that was some generalization about the top 100 words in English! What are the most frequently used words in English, anyway? And do they really come from Old English? To check it out yourself, follow these directions.

1. Choose one page of text in a book. Use any book that is primarily written in complete sentences (so, not a dictionary, for example) and is written in English.

2. Count how many times each word appears and keep tabs. You might want to use tally marks. This won't exactly give you the top 100 most frequently used words in English, but it will give you an idea of some words that are used pretty often.

3. Use a dictionary to look up the most frequently used words you found. Check out the etymological information in the entry (the part that tells what language the word comes from).

4. Compare your findings with someone else's, if possible. What are the similarities? The differences?

(Answers are on page xv.)

Getting back to the history of English. . . . In about A.D. 600, the language began to change because St. Augustine came to Britain, bringing Christianity and a lot of Latin words. People started learning to write English, and so English spelling was invented.

But then more invasions brought more new words into English. The Viking invasions began in the late 700s, bringing Danish words. Then, in 1066, came William the Conqueror and the Normans, bringing French words. After a couple of hundred years, the differences that resulted from the addition of French had become so great that the change in the language has a name. We call the mixture of Old English with French that was spoken starting in the early 1200s **Middle English**. Just to let you know how that influence has lasted, about 40 percent of all English words used today have French origins.

The rediscovery of Greek and Latin classics in the period of the Renaissance (1300s to 1600s) and the introduction of the printing press in the 1400s brought many new words to England.

But those aren't all the sources for English!! Not by a long shot. Here's a sampling of fairly common English words and their sources:

Word	Language of Origin	Word	Language of Origin
algebra	Arabic	klutz	Yiddish
boomerang	Dhaurk (Australian Aborigine language)	skunk	Algonquian
cafeteria	Spanish	pizza	Italian
chipmunk	Ojibwa	tepee	Dakota
futon	Japanese	wok	Chinese
ketchup or catsup	Malay	yak	Tibetan

All these new additions to the language kept things very unsettled (or interesting, depending on how you look at it) until the mid-1700s, when English spelling began to become standardized as the result of the publication of a definitive dictionary by Samuel Johnson—and this is when **Modern English** began.

As the language continued to evolve and all the influences we've mentioned continued, dictionaries began to take account of multiple pronunciations and spellings, placing the most frequently used or preferred version first.

It's finally done.

BRAIN TICKLERS
Set #2 English Word Etymologies

1. Look at this list of ten common English words that have come into English from another language. Use a dictionary to look up each word's etymology. The dictionary will begin with the language from which the word came most recently and work back to the language of ultimate origin. Briefly tell in what language the word began and how it traveled into English.

artichoke	boss	cooky or cookie	jungle	oboe
raccoon	robot	sponge	tea	teak

2. Choose a word that you think may have come into English from another language. Check in a dictionary to see if you are right. Keep checking until you find one. Write down the word and the language it originally started in.

(Answers are on page xv.)

Now that you know a little about the sources of English, it will be easier for you to understand why there are multiple patterns of spelling in modern English. Each language of origin has its own rules for representing sounds with symbols. In addition, the pronunciation of English has changed over time. So sounds are not represented by letters in English in a one-to-one correspondence. (We'll talk more about this beginning in Chapter 3.) This book will help you spell English words by calling your attention to the patterns of spelling and by helping you understand what you can expect from English words.

BRAIN TICKLERS—THE ANSWERS

Set #1, page xi

Answers will vary depending on the material you have chosen. Possible response: The most frequently used word in the first section of this Introduction (pages vii–x; 1030 words) is (can you guess?) *the*. It appears 62 times. And guess what! It's from Old English. In fact, all of the 15 most frequently used words in this section are from Old English except for one: *spelling* is from Old French. Here are the rest of the top 15 words:

to 34 times	**is** 18 times
you 28 times	**that** 14 times
of 28 times	**with** 11 times
and 26 times	**for** 11 times
English 24 times	**words** 9 times
a 24 times	**we** 9 times
in 22 times	

Set #2, page xiv

1. Answers may vary depending on the dictionary used.
   artichoke   Arabic to Old Spanish to Italian to English
   boss   Germanic to Middle Dutch to Dutch to English
   cooky or cookie   Middle Dutch to Dutch to English
   jungle   Sanskrit to Hindi and Marathi to English
   oboe   French to Italian to English
   raccoon   Algonquin to English
   robot   Czech to English
   sponge   Greek to Latin to Old English to Middle English
   tea   Ancient Chinese to Amoy to Malay to Dutch to English
   teak   Malayalam to Portuguese to English

2. Answers will vary. Possible responses:
   café Turkish
   curry Tamil
   galore Irish Gaelic
   galoshes Old French
   knack Middle Dutch
   mesa Latin
   omelet Latin

   pharaoh Egyptian
   sierra Latin
   soy Mandarin Chinese
   squirrel Greek
   taco Spanish
   tortilla Late Latin

Part One

HOW TO SPELL PROPERLY IN ALL TIMES AND SEASONS

CHAPTER ONE

Spelling in the 21st Century

In the Introduction, I pointed out that there is often more than one correct and standard way to spell a word. We reviewed the fact that even reliable dictionaries differ on the "proper" spelling of standard English. But there is another reason why a word can have multiple spellings. Sometimes, different spellings are used for different purposes. We'll discuss both of these elements of spelling in this chapter, reviewing some of the circumstances that can make particular spellings correct, useful, or desirable. Also included are hints for helping you make good spelling choices.

DICTIONARY DIFFERENCES

People are fond of pointing out that even Shakespeare, that great master of the written word, was known to spell his own last name in different ways at different times. For years and years, nobody thought that spelling the same word in different ways was such a problem. Spelling of English started to become regular in the 1600s to 1700s, and became much more standardized with Samuel Johnson's dictionary, as we mentioned in the Introduction.

But would you believe that after several hundred years of trying to regularize our spelling, we still haven't managed? In the 1970s—not that long ago in the history of English— Lee C. Deighton compared four of the major American English dictionaries and found considerable disagreement about the "right" way to spell several thousand common English words.

Not only do the dictionaries all offer multiple correct spellings, but they often disagree with each other about how to spell the words.

Here are some examples. How do you spell the word we usually say when we part company? Well, according to Deighton's study, it could be *good-by*, *goodby*, *good-bye*, or *goodbye*. If you're scared, you might be *chickenhearted*, or you might be *chicken-hearted*. That healthy stuff you ate for lunch might be *yogurt*, *yoghurt*, or *yoghourt*. And a song that is traditionally sung to a newly married couple takes the cake! It can be spelled *shivaree*, *charivaree*, *chivaree*, *chivari*, or *charivari*. Is that confusing, or what?

BRAIN TICKLERS
Set #3 Multiple Correct Spellings

1. Here are some words that have more than one correct spelling in English. Using a dictionary at home, in the library, at school, or on the Internet, find at least one alternate spelling for each word. Record your findings. Hint: The spellings below are from *The American Heritage Dictionary*, so you might want to try using a different dictionary.

   clear-headed   per cent   teen-age
   corn flakes   retrorocket

2. How many different spellings can you find for the word *boogieman*? Write down the names of the dictionaries or other sources you used and the spellings you found.

(Answers are on page 32.)

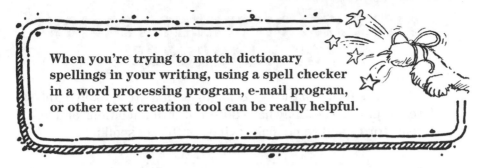

When you're trying to match dictionary spellings in your writing, using a spell checker in a word processing program, e-mail program, or other text creation tool can be really helpful.

SPELLING FOR DIFFERENT PURPOSES

On the title page for this chapter, you can see an example of a student making different spelling choices for different purposes. In the two different communications—one, schoolwork; the other, a text message—he is shown using different spellings for *great*, *brother*, and *laugh out loud* that are appropriate to the different situations.

Besides choosing a spelling that matches at least one dictionary if you're doing schoolwork (your teacher may tell you exactly which dictionary to use), there are three key factors you can consider to help you decide which of several correct spellings to choose:

- Consider your location. What spellings are expected from people who live where you do? See the section below on DIALECTS (different regional forms of the same language) for more information.
- Consider your audience. What will your audience readily understand and not consider "improper"? See the section below on REGISTERS (standards for how formal or informal language is) for more information.
- Consider the form that you're writing. What approach to spelling makes sense for the number of pages or number of characters you have available? See the section below on GENRES (different forms of writing and speaking) for more information.

DIALECTS: DIFFERENT VERSIONS OF A LANGUAGE

Dialects are forms of the same language that are spoken in different regions. They may have different pronunciations and different words, and some dialects have different spellings.

When in Rome, do as the Romans do

The saying "When in Rome, do as the Romans do" suggests that it is often useful to adapt to the expectations and standards of the place you're in. What is correct and standard in one place may differ from what is correct and standard somewhere else. Different locations may have different styles of dress, different foods, different customs, and differences in their use of language, including spelling. If you want to fit in, you follow along with the local rules.

Versions of English are spoken by people in the United States, Canada, the United Kingdom, Australia, and New Zealand as a first language, and as a first or second language in many other countries. When the same language has different versions, these versions are called *dialects*. The English language has two main dialects: American English and British English. American English is used in the United States, and British English is used in the other countries named above.*

There are some important differences between the two dialects. For one thing, British and American English are pronounced differently in general. You can probably tell a speaker of British English from a speaker of American English as soon as he or she speaks. In addition, some particular words are pronounced in alternate ways. The contrasts are mainly in vowel sounds and stress. In this chart, with the bold letters showing the stressed syllable, you can see pronunciations of four words that sound strikingly different, but are written exactly the same.

	glacier	schedule	privacy	harass
American English Pronunciation	**glā** shûr	**skĕd** yo͞ol	**prī** və sē	hə **răs**
British English Pronunciation	**glă** sī ə	**shĕd** yo͞ol	**prĭ** və sē	**hâ** rəs

There are also some vocabulary distinctions, with different words being used for the same thing. For example, what is called an *elevator* in American English is called a *lift* in British English.

But for our purposes, the most important difference between British and American English is the spelling of certain words.

What this means is that where you are in the world can actually change whether you've spelled words correctly!

---

*British English has some differences in different locations, but since our focus is American English, we're not going to go into them here.

For example, if you lived in Detroit, Michigan, where American English is the standard, it would be correct to write this in a school paper:

> My adventure began suddenly. I was standing on the curb in front of the new health center, which had been painted my least favorite color, gray. It was then that I spotted the airplane flying low overhead.

Across the river—about one-half mile away in Windsor, Ontario—the Canadian form of British English is the standard. Here, you would be expected to spell a number of words in the passage differently.

> My adventure began suddenly. I was standing on the kerb in front of the new health centre, which had been painted my least favourite colour, grey. It was then that I spotted the aeroplane flying low overhead.

Do you see all six differences?

Dialects in Cyberspace

It used to be rare that a young American would come across British English spellings. For a long time, communication with people who were not nearby was difficult and rare. When this was the case, pretty much every time a person read, they saw their own dialect. The spellings that they were supposed to use were reinforced by seeing them frequently.

This separation of written dialects began to change with affordable mail, which allows communication between people who may be far apart. Today, the Internet allows people through-out the world to communicate with each other depending on access to technology, rather than location. Due to the Internet, reading the words of someone who uses British English has become far more common for a young American, and vice versa.

Today, it is not only easy to find British English online, but there may be nothing obvious to let you know that it is British English, rather than American English. You can easily find online newspapers, books, and stores from other countries. In addition, people young and old from all around the world may post to the same online forums, add comments to the same blogs, follow the same Facebook or MySpace pages, and send each other various types of messages, from e-mails to tweets. All in all, it's far more likely these days that young people have seen different correct spellings from another dialect than it used to be. As a result, when it comes time to write the words that are spelled differ-ently in the two dialects, it might be difficult to recall which is correct. *Favorite* is not obviously better than *favourite*. *Centre* and *center* both look as if they're pronounced /SEN tər/.

Spelling books for American English didn't used to pay much, if any, attention to British English. This made sense at the time, since young Americans weren't seeing it. In the past, discussing British English would just have added confusion. Now that we *do* see British English spelling fairly frequently, calling attention to the differences can help you be aware of the types of words in which differences are most often found. If you know the main differences, you can avoid choosing a correct spelling that just doesn't happen to be the correct spelling for where you are.

It is important to note that in both British and American English, proper nouns (the names of people, places, and things) should keep their original spellings. For example, *Sydney Harbour*, where the famous Sydney Opera House is situated, is always written with the British spelling of *harbour*, no matter where you are.

Key American English and British English Spelling Differences

Knowing four key differences in British English and American English spelling will help you avoid the type of spelling errors that are a right spelling in the wrong location.

- *o* **vs.** *ou* A number of British words have *ou* where there is only an *o* in American English.
- *er* **vs.** *re* A number of British words end *re* where American English words end with *er*.
- *ce* **vs.** *se* A number of British words end *ce* where American English words end *se*.
- *s* **vs.** *z:* (*ise / ize*; *yse / yze*; and *isation / ization*) A number of British words use an *s* in these endings where American English uses a *z*.

BRAIN TICKLERS
Set #4 Sort British and American English

These word pairs follow the differences explained above. Write each word in the side of the chart where it belongs to show if the spelling is proper to American English or British English.

recognise	recognize	globalization	globalisation	litre	liter
license	licence	apologize	apologise	humour	humor
mold	mould	analyze	analyse	realisation	realization
sceptre	scepter	organisation	organization	emphasise	emphasize
kilometre	kilometer	honor	honour	paralyze	paralyse
catalyse	catalyze	defence	defense	offense	offence

American English	British English	American English	British English

(Answers are on page 32.)

REGISTERS: FORMAL AND INFORMAL LANGUAGE

Registers are levels of formality ranging from very informal to very formal. Every reader of this book is so used to switching language registers that it's not something you may consciously think about. But taking a moment to consider it may be helpful in making some of your spelling choices more conscious. Since many teachers don't want to see informal language used in schoolwork, getting a handle on this could prove really helpful.

Formal and informal language and spelling

The registers of a dialect or language are its levels of formal and informal language. Some people talk as if there were just two different things: formal and informal. Actually, there are many different levels of both formal and informal language. Varieties of formal language are often used in courtrooms; churches, synagogues, and mosques; government offices; and many companies, for example. Informal language is often used at home and at playgrounds, parks, shopping malls, and vacation spots.

People, as well as places, help determine how formal or informal a language situation is. Classrooms, for example, may range from formal to informal, depending on both the teacher and the school, but school assignments frequently require more formal language. It is also more usual to use formal language with people one doesn't know well, older adults, and people who hold special offices. On the other hand, it is more common to use informal language with family and friends.

Formal and informal language differ in several ways. They may be used to communicate about different topics, use different words, have different grammar and mechanics rules, and employ different spellings.

There's a famous poem that jokes about the trouble that can arise if a person makes a register choice that his or her audience doesn't agree with:

Don't say *ain't*
Or your mother will faint
And your father will fall in a bucket of paint
And your brother will die
And your sister will cry
And your cat will call the FBI.

(Some people end the poem with the line, "And your cat and dog will say goodbye.")

BRAIN TICKLERS
Set #5 Consider Language Choices

1. In your own words, tell what the poem means.

2. Describe a time or place in which someone used language that was considered too informal. (Names can be changed to protect the innocent ;^)

(Answers are on page 33.)

In the poem, the family clearly overreacts. But language registers are taken very seriously by some people and in some situations. Even if you don't agree that it's important, it's good to know how to communicate in different registers. One good reason to learn this is that your grades may suffer if you use informal language and spelling in school. Another good reason is that when you communicate in the expected register, your audience will be focused on what you say, not on how you are saying it.

Some people defend using language that others may find offensive or inappropriate by saying that they're expressing themselves honestly. It helps to make a distinction between self-expression, on the one hand, and communication, on the other hand. When you're expressing yourself, you're not concerned with anyone else. When you're communicating, there's an audience for your words. In this case, you're trying to convey something to someone else, so taking his or her standards into account is a fundamental part of the process. If you choose to ignore your audience, your communication may not be successful.

When you're talking about something that's important to you, getting people focused on your meaning, not your spelling, helps you to make your point effectively.

Formality, Informality, and Spelling

Different levels of formality have different vocabulary words, different pronunciations, and different spellings. For example, if you were trying to fit your communication to a specific register, there are certain choices you'd probably make.

Register Differences	Examples
Vocabulary Words	You most likely wouldn't use the word *heretofore* or *whither* or *antidisestablishmentarianism* in an informal situation (in fact, you might never use those words!). In a formal situation, you probably wouldn't use slang.
Pronunciation	You very likely wouldn't use *gonna* instead of *going to* (or other informal pronunciations) in formal speaking or writing.
Spelling	You probably wouldn't use *ez* instead of *easy* (or other shortened spellings) in a formal situation.

If you have friends or classmates who are non-native speakers of English, you can help them understand which words, pronunciations, and spellings in American English are best saved for only informal or only formal use.

It's pretty likely that all of your spelling instruction so far has been in the formal spelling of words, rather than the informal spelling. But sometimes seeing two options side by side can be useful to help you note the differences. When you know what the choices are, it's easier to make sure you use each spelling in settings where it fits.

Here is a chart of words that often have a different informal spelling and formal spelling:

Formal Spelling	Informal Spelling
doughnut	donut
night	nite
light	lite
highway	hiway
socks	sox
thanks	thanx
through	thru
of	o'
and	'n'
easy	ez
enough	enuf

The type of informal spelling shown in the chart is sometimes called *simplified spelling*. You can see why if you compare the number of letters in the words in the right-hand column to their match in the left-hand column. The words on the right use fewer letters. They use an alternative spelling that produces the same sound so that people will still recognize the word. The pattern *ough* seems to be high on the list for replacement. In *donut*, where the *gh* is silent, *ough* is replaced by *o*. In *thru*, where the *gh* is also silent, *ough* is replaced by *u*. In *enough*, where the *gh* isn't silent, *ough* is replaced by *uf*.

BRAIN TICKLERS
Set #6 Multiple Correct Spelling

For each pair of words, explain how the informal spelling simplifies the formal spelling. If you need more room, copy the chart to another piece of paper.

Formal Spelling	Informal Spelling	Explanation
night	nite	
light	lite	
highway	hiway	
socks	sox	
thanks	thanx	
of	o'	
and	'n'	
easy	ez	

(Answers are on page 33.)

Exceptions: Quotation and Characterization

There are two important exceptions to the general guidelines about fitting your spelling to how formal the occasion is. The first is when you are quoting someone in nonfiction. The second is when you are creating a character in fiction, poetry, or drama, for example.

When you are quoting someone, whether the words were spoken or written, your greatest obligation is to truth. In some cases, like research studies, it is common to find informal

19

quotations imbedded in formal prose. Imagine, for example, a research paper by a specialist in education writing about student use of text messages:

> In the study carried out at Springfield High School, seventy-three ninth graders volunteered to share their text messages and tweets for the month of September. Communications were rated for informal markers by two researchers. The following passage illustrates some of the characteristic usages:
>
> gr8 joke, bro!!!! LOL!!!

Because of the topic, readers will not be surprised to find informal prose, including nonstandard spelling, included in the example texts in this study. The study wouldn't be of much value if it did *not* include examples of informal prose that are spelled exactly as in the original.

News reports may also quote an important authority, newsmaker, or witness to an event using informal language. As in research studies, in news reports it is acceptable to have a different language register in quotations and in the prose surrounding them. But in news reports, unlike research studies, there may be another factor at work. Newspapers, news magazines, and online news sources have standards for prose that is suitable for their readers. Like them, you have an obligation to your audience, and it can sometimes be a challenge to navigate a path between truthful quotation and writing suitably for your readers.

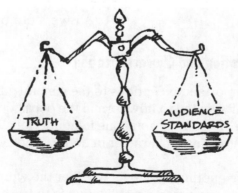

If you need to quote formal words in an informal setting, the words may sound stilted, but that is usually not a problem. But an informal quote in a formal situation can have several problems. It may include words that the audience will potentially find offensive. It may also include words that are spelled in a way that will prevent the audience from knowing what they mean. Misspellings or informal spellings may occur, too. If an informal quote is important to whatever you are writing, and the writing is in a formal situation, then you have several choices:

- You may be able to paraphrase to avoid other problems. When you paraphrase a quotation, you give a true sense of what was said without using the exact words.
- If one or more words that you think may be objectionable to your audience were used in the quotation, you may be able to get around this by omitting some of the letters. For example, you could spell them with just the first letter and asterisks or dashes to substitute for the other letters. This helps you be true to the person you are quoting while acknowledging the standards of your audience. This practice is over 130 years old.

- If you don't think the audience will understand the meaning of words in the quotation because of the way they are spelled, you can put an explanation in brackets or create a footnote. For example,

  [TMI stands for "too much information." It means that someone has over-shared.]

- If the person you are quoting has misspelled a word, what you should do depends on the circumstances. One approach is to put [sic] after the misspelled word. The brackets indicate that the error is in the original quote and that *sic* is an editorial comment, not a part of the original quote. Another approach is to replace the misspelling with the correct spelling in brackets.

Let's say you need to quote this material:

  "Stop hating on him. It was all a big misteak."

The two alternatives are:

  "Stop hating on him. It was all a big misteak [sic]."

  "Stop hating on him. It was all a big [mistake]."

The first is a "letter of the law" approach, preserving strict accuracy. The second clearly shows the change, but omits the mistake, so may be kinder. If you are not sure which to use, check with a trusted source.

- Sometimes it just doesn't make sense to render words with formal spelling, because it would make the quotation ridiculous. For example, if someone said,

  "Whaddaya mean? I ain't gonna give her no job."

spelling it as:

  "What do you mean? I ain't going to give her no job."

creates a strange mix of formal and informal that seems fake. True, the words are now all spelled as one would expect for formal prose, but some things about the sentence still are not formal. *Ain't* is not considered an appropriate word for formal use (*am not* is preferred). *No* creates a double negative, frowned upon in formal writing. In other words, to really make it formal, you would have to change it to:

"What do you mean? I am not going to give her a job."

But those grammar and vocabulary changes go beyond the bounds of what you are allowed to do with a quotation. If you have a complicated situation like this, make no changes, paraphrase, or, if that's not acceptable, ask for advice.

- In other situations, as well, you may be able to explain the situation to the person you're writing for (your teacher, for example) and ask for guidance.

Now let's turn to the case of characterization. If you are creating a fictional character or a character in a drama, it is important to convey the character's use of language, including spelling. This is another case in which the approach of making the language fit the usual standard for formal prose may need to fall by the wayside. The techniques suggested above for quotations may work for similar issues in creating your character's speech or writing. If you're working on a school assignment, it's a good idea to check with your teacher about how to go about this.

GENRES: DIFFERENT TYPES OF WRITING

Genres are different types of writing, and being able to make distinctions between genres can help you avoid using a correct spelling in the wrong situation.

Spelling to fit the form

The word *genres* refers to the different types of writing that there are. Examples of genres include long forms like court decisions, legislation, white papers, and dissertations. These works tend to be formal. Short genres include limericks, Power-Point slides, and advertisements. These may be formal or informal, depending on the subject matter. E-mails and fiction may be long or short and formal or informal—they adapt to many purposes and situations.

There are four genres of writing that are very short and mostly informal and often include alternative spellings. They are tweets—the messages sent via Twitter, vanity license plates (see top of p. 25), trade names (names of companies, like TOYSЯUS), and text (or SMS—Short Message Service) messages.

BRAIN TICKLERS
Set #7 Translate Vanity License Plates

Use the clues of design, spacing, spelling, and sound to translate each of these license plates into English. If you're having trouble figuring them out, look ahead to the hints about abbreviations on pages 29–30.

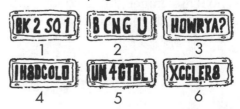

BK 2 SQ 1	B CNG U	HOWRYA?
1	2	3
IH8DCOLD	UN4GTBL	XCCLER8
4	5	6

(Answers are on page 33.)

The way spelling is used in these four genres differs from other short genres, like haiku, for example. A haiku—a poem that only has 17 syllables—is usually written in formal English, with everything spelled according to the standards. A tweet, license plate, trade name, or text message often uses inventive shortenings and respellings of words to enable fitting as much information as possible into the short space available. It may also ignore some of the traditional rules of grammar, mechanics, and style, using sentence fragments and skipping punctuation, for example.

What Are Generic Expectations?

The collection of expectations we have for the grammar, spelling, mechanics, etc., connected with each writing genre are called *generic expectations*. (Notice how the final *e* and *r* in *genre* switch places when the noun is changed to an adjective form.) Many genres have somewhat specific generic expectations. One of the important parts of choosing between multiple correct spellings is using spellings that fit the generic expectations for what we're writing.

For example, take a look back at the chapter opener on page 3. The student wrote these sentences as part of a school assignment:

> My brother texted a really great joke to me. It was so funny that even though I was in the library, I started laughing out loud.

This communication is only 129 characters. It could easily fit the character limit of a tweet (140 characters) or a text message (160 characters). But it doesn't have the kind of grammar, style, or spelling that are usually found in those types of communication. It just doesn't fit. It violates generic expectations, and if you received a tweet or text message like this, you would probably think it was really weird.

On the other hand, we have the text message:

> gr8 joke, bro!!!! LOL!!!

The use of sentence fragments, nonstandard spelling, and abbreviation would violate the generic expectations of formal prose, unless—as we showed above—it was used in quotation or characterization.

When a genre itself doesn't have clear expectations—like e-mail or fiction—the expectations are created by the situation. In cases like this, you consider both the audience and the subject matter. For example, an e-mail to a potential employer is likely to be formal, whereas an e-mail to your best friend is likely to be informal. A story that takes place in a courtroom will definitely have some formal language, whereas a story about a teenager teaching a robot the basics of 21st century life might be mainly informal.

Spelling in Text Messages, IMs, and Tweets

Some people refer to the adaptive spelling used in text messages and tweets as "misspelling" or "wrong." Another way to look at it is an appropriate spelling for some situations, but not for *all* situations. Two points follow. First, it's useful to know the conventions of these short messages in order to use them effectively. Second, it's useful to know how to switch between this type of informal prose and the more formal prose expected in other situations, such as school and work.

There are, as mentioned above, differences of vocabulary and grammar rules, as well as spelling. Since this is a spelling book, we'll focus on spelling differences, which fall into five categories: contractions, initialisms, acronyms, other abbreviations, and emoticons.

- **Contractions** A contraction, as we will discuss further in Chapter 6 (page 145), is a shortened form of two or three words that are combined, with one or more letters replaced by an apostrophe. Contractions are frequent in informal prose and great in text messages and tweets because they save space. In nearly all contractions, one of the combined words is a verb. Note that not all words with apostrophes are contractions, though. Apostrophes can appear in names and in possessives.

  In some types of formal prose, contractions are frowned on. In such cases, spelling the words out fully, rather than using contractions, is the fix. One exception is *o'clock*, which comes from the phrase "of the clock," and—despite being a contraction—is acceptable in any register.

- **Initialisms** An initialism, as we will discuss further in Chapter 6 (page 142), is a shortened phrase in which only the initial letter of words is used. It has no periods and is pronounced by saying each of the letters. An example is *ROTFL*, which stands for *Rolling On The Floor Laughing*. Shortening a whole phrase down to just a few letters is a great strategy for informal prose and especially short forms like text messages and tweets.

  There are also some initialisms that are abbreviations of phrases that are a bit more formal to start with. Examples include:

  > afaik—as far as I know
  > fyi—for your information
  > btw—by the way
  > asap—as soon as possible

Unlike ROTFL, these are more likely to be used in semiformal genres, like business e-mails.

Standard initialisms, such as company names (IBM for International Business Machines), medical terminology (HIV for Human Immunodeficiency Virus), educational degrees (BA for Bachelor of Arts), and time (PM for Post

Meridiem; CE for Common Era) are accepted in formal prose. All except the ones for time are usually used only after the full, written-out form is given. After the full name is given, the initialism follows in parentheses. The next time, the initialism alone can be used.

> Anorexia nervosa is an example of an eating disorder (ED). Treating EDs is the subject of several new books.

Because some initialisms are acceptable in formal prose, a blanket rule won't work. Deciding which initialisms might be acceptable may require actively thinking about the words that are "hidden" by the initials. Sometimes, initialisms can be considered objectionable because they actually refer to private body parts or swear words, but when you're looking at the initialism, this isn't obvious because all you see is the initials, not the words they stand for. It's another reason, however, that an initialism may not be appropriate for a formal setting.

- **Acronyms** An acronym is an initialism that is pronounced as if it were a word. An example is *scuba* (Self-Contained Underwater Breathing Apparatus). Acronyms are useful in text messages and tweets for the same reasons that other abbreviations are, but for formal use, they can have all the same issues that initialisms do, plus one more. Since they are pronounced as words, people may be unaware of what words the acronym is "concealing" behind the initials. This could result in unintentionally using a word that has an informal, or even offensive, meaning.

  The U.S. military goes a little beyond acronyms, stringing together portions of words to shorten long phrases in a way that makes them pronounceable. It may make sense to them, but it's not always easy to understand for people outside. For example, ADCOMSUBORDCOMPHIBSPAC, the abbreviation for Administrative Command, Amphibious Forces, Pacific Fleet Subordinate Command, is so long that you might think it needs its own abbreviation!

BRAIN TICKLERS
Set #8 Research and Categorize Acronyms

Research these ten acronyms that are pronounced as words to find out the phrases
that they stand for. Fill in the chart and
check under "Informal" if you think a
word is best reserved for "informal" use.

Word	Meaning	Informal?
RAM		
Laser		
MUBAR		
AIDS		
WYSIWYG		
SADD		
POTUS		
w00t		
NIMBY		
FINE		

(Answers are on page 34.)

- **Other Abbreviations** There are many other types of
  abbreviations, some of which use initials and some of
  which don't.

  - The abbreviation *IOU*, for example, short for *I owe you*,
    uses the initials of the first two words, but substitutes a
    letter with a name that sounds like the last word, rather
    than using the *Y*.
  - The abbreviation *gr8* substitutes a single-digit number
    with a name that sounds /āt/ for three letters that make
    an identical sound in the word *great*.

- The abbreviation *ur* for *your* omits the first two letters of the word and relies on the letter name for the *u*, but the usual pronunciation of *r*.
- The abbreviation *4* can replace the word *for*, saving two characters.
- The abbreviation @ has a special meaning in tweets. The symbol literally means "at," and it is used in place of *to* as an indication of who is being addressed in a tweet.

@EdReinvented Thanx 4 spelling tips!

(@ also has other uses on Twitter, for example, in retweets.) It cannot, however, be substituted for *to* in formal communication.

Notice that in all of these cases, you don't just read the word as usual, finding a pronunciation for the letter pattern. Instead, the words require you to be flexible in how you get meaning from spelling. As a result, these cases can all be considered playful uses of language. If an abbreviation is playful, you can be fairly certain that it is considered informal and not appropriate for formal prose.

BRAIN TICKLERS
Set #9 Explain Abbreviations

Following the explanations above, explain how each of these abbreviations works.

Phrase	Abbreviation	Explanation
Bye for now.	B4N	
Chuckle and grin	C&G	
Talk to you later.	TLK 2 U L8R	
You've got to be kidding!	UG2BK	
Starbucks	*$	

(Answers are on page 35.)

BRAIN TICKLERS
Set #10 Translate Emoticons

Translate each emoticon into standard English.

Emoticon	Standard English Alternative
:'-(	
:-&	
>8-O	
8-o	
;^)	

(Answers are on page 34.)

- **Emoticons** An emoticon is an image that shows an emotion or attitude and is made from keyboard characters. Most are created sideways and require turning the paper 90° clockwise to appear right-side up.
  Examples include:

;^) or ;)	winking smile
:^) or :)	smile
:^(or :(	frown
8-o	surprised
>8-O	very angry
:-&	confused
:'-(	crying

While these can be very important in marking the tone of communication (like sarcasm or humor), they fall into the playful category and are not accepted in formal prose. In formal prose, if an emotional marker is needed, it is expected to be spelled out in standard English.

See Chapter 6, page 142 for more information on spelling abbreviations that are commonly used in formal writing.

BRAIN TICKLERS—THE ANSWERS

Set #3, page 6

1. Answers will vary depending on the dictionaries and the words chosen. Here is a possible set of responses:

   Merriam Webster's 11th edition spellings
clearheaded	percent	teenage
cornflakes	retro-rocket	

2. Answers will vary depending on the dictionary or dictionaries chosen. Here is a possible response:

boogieman	boogeyman	bogeyman
boogyman	bogyman	

Set #4, page 13

American English	British English
recognize	recognise
globalization	globalisation
liter	litre
license	licence
apologize	apologise
humor	humour
mold	mould
analyze	analyse
realization	realisation

American English	British English
scepter	sceptre
organization	organisation
emphasize	emphasise
kilometer	kilometre
honor	honour
paralyze	paralyse
catalyze	catalyse
defense	defence
offense	offence

Set #5, page 16

1. Possible responses:

   - The overreaction of the family, down to the cat, is meant to make fun of people who are prissy about informal language: it's really not that bad!

   - The poem exaggerates the response to the use of informal language to provide a playful reminder that people should consider their audience when they write or speak.

2. Answers will vary.

Set #6, page 19

Formal Spelling	Informal Spelling	Explanation
night	nite	*ght* is replaced with *te*
light	lite	*ght* is replaced with *te*
highway	hiway	*gh* is dropped
socks	sox	*cks* is replaced with *x*
thanks	thanx	*ks* is replaced with *x*
of	o'	*f* is replaced with an apostrophe
and	'n'	*a* and *d* are replaced with apostrophes
easy	ez	*ea* is replaced with *e* and *sy* is replaced with *z*

Set #7, page 24

1. Back to square one.
2. Be seeing you.
3. How are you?
4. I hate the cold.
5. Unforgettable
6. Accelerate

Set #8, page 29

Possible responses:

Word	Meaning	Informal?
RAM	Random-Access Memory	
laser	Light Amplification by Simulated Emission of Radiation	
MUBAR	Messed Up Beyond All Recognition	✓
AIDS	Acquired Immune Deficiency Syndrome	
WYSIWYG	What You See Is What You Get	✓
SADD	Students Against Destructive Decisions (formerly Students Against Drunk Driving)	
POTUS	President Of The United States	
w00t	We Owned the Other Team	✓
NIMBY	Not In My Back Yard	✓
FINE	Freaked out, Insecure, Neurotic, and Emotional	✓

Set #9, page 30—see p. 35.

Set #10, page 31

Possible responses:

Emoticon	Standard English Alternative
:'–(	I am very sad about what is happening.
:–&	This is confusing to me.
>8–O	The situation has really upset me.
8–o	I was not expecting that!
;^)	I'm joking!

Set #9, page 30

Possible responses:

Phrase	Abbreviation	Explanation
Bye for now.	B4N	*B* and *N* are initials. The number *4*, which is pronounced the same way as *for*, replaces *for*.
Chuckle and grin	C&G	*C* and *G* are initials. The ampersand symbol, which means "and," replaces *and*.
Talk to you later.	TLK 2 U L8R	*Talk* is abbreviated by omitting the vowel and *2*, which is pronounced the same way as *to*, replaces *to*. *U*, the name of which is pronounced the same way as you, replaces *you*. The first and last letters of *later* are kept, and *8*, the name of which is pronounced the same way as the three middle letters, replaces them.
You've got to be kidding!	UG2BK	*G*, *B*, and *K* are initials. *U*, the name of which is pronounced the same as *you*, is substituted for *you've* with the verb *have* ignored. *2*, which is pronounced the same way as *to*, replaces *to*.
Starbucks	*$	The asterisk is a kind of star and stands for the first syllable. The dollar sign stands for "money," an informal synonym of which is *bucks*.

Part Two

AMERICAN ENGLISH SPELLING

CHAPTER TWO

Overview of English Spelling

ENGLISH SPELLING: THE BASICS

This section will get you warmed up for the kind of work you'll be doing in the rest of the book. It is based on the idea that there is a relationship between what you see when you look at a word written down, and what you hear when a word is spoken aloud. Because this relationship is not always clear, sometimes you have to analyze a word to understand it. Starting with this chapter, unless otherwise indicated, *English spelling* refers to *American English* spelling.

Nobody is ever finished learning to spell

It's important to realize that learning to spell is a process that isn't complete for anyone. As you've seen, even the experts can't agree on how to spell a large number of words correctly. In addition, new words are constantly being added to English as people create new concepts and invent equipment with new names and as new slang terms are invented. Besides that, as each of us learns new subject areas and skills, we need a new vocabulary so we can talk about our experience, so our personal vocabularies keep expanding.

It's true that some people have an easier time spelling than others. But spelling is something that everyone has to pay attention to. So now let's look at the way we learn to spell.

We start with sound

Think about how people learn language. Maybe you have a younger brother or sister, or maybe a baby lives next door to you. Do they start off learning English by trying to write words? Of course not! They listen to people speak English, and they begin by learning that the sounds they hear can be understood as words, each of which MEANS something. To them, *dog* is a group of sounds that refers to a furry, four-legged beast that licks their faces.

And that's the key to thinking about words—words are sounds written down. After you figure this out—after you understand that written words are a code for the sounds of words spoken aloud—you can learn to read and write. And eventually you get to the point at which you realize that if you want to be understood easily, you have to write *k-n-o-w*, and not *k-n-o* or *n-o-e*.

But this is where English can get confusing, because if you want to write the word *boat*, you spell the same sound that you hear in *no* but with the letters *o-a*; and if you want to write the word *doe*, you spell it *o-e*. The job of this book is to help you figure out the different ways to spell the sounds you hear by giving you rules and strategies. Then you can understand and remember the different patterns for recording the sounds of English. And the most important tool for making sound patterns in writing is, of course, the alphabet.

The alphabet

Okay. We've got the English alphabet with 26 letters. And each letter, by itself, can represent one or more sounds. (For example, you probably know by now that the vowels can have a long or short pronunciation and that the letter *c* can be pronounced like the letter *k* or like the letter *s*, depending on the context.)

But when you put letters together, you can record some sounds that you can't record with a single letter, and you can also duplicate some sounds that you could already make with one letter. For example, the letters *ow* spell a sound that you can't spell with one letter, but *ph* can indicate the same sound as *f* does by itself.

And when you put some letters next to others, the sound changes. (For example, an *r* following a vowel can change the pronunciation of the vowel.)

This sounds really complicated. And some people get really upset about it. The British playwright George Bernard Shaw scoffed that you could just as well spell *fish* as *ghoti* if you used *gh* from *rough*, *o* from *women*, and *ti* from *nation*.

The problem of spelling was so important to Shaw, that when he died, he left A LOT of his money for the purpose of trying to reform English spelling so it would have one, and only one, symbol for each sound. But the old 26-letter alphabet is still being used.

BRAIN TICKLERS
Set #11 Make Up a Spelling

Make up a new spelling of a word the same way George Bernard Shaw did. Share it with a classmate or friend, and see if he or she can figure out what word you spelled.

(Answers are on page 63.)

BRAIN TICKLERS
Set #12 Evaluate Shaw's Alphabet

1. Look at this chart of the alphabet developed to meet Shaw's requirements for a new alphabet. It was created through a competition that closed on January 1, 1959.

The alphabet has 55 letters and eight vowel markers. Each letter represents one, and only one sound. What do you think the value of such an alphabet could be? Do you think replacing the 26-letter alphabet with the one shown here would work? Write a paragraph explaining your ideas.

2. Go back to the page with the chapter title (page 39) and use the chart to help you figure out what it says on the billboard. Write your answer.

(Answers are on page 63.)

The patterns

As we've already pointed out, some sounds can be spelled in more than one way and some letters can spell more than one sound. This makes English more complicated than, say, Spanish, in which each letter has just one pronunciation (on the whole). In this section, we're going to take a brief but in-depth overview of the spelling patterns of American English. You don't need to focus a lot of attention on rare or unusual spellings, but it will be helpful if you know they exist. Then we'll start over with the basics, offering a fuller explanation of elements of spelling that are handled briefly here.

BRAIN TICKLERS
Set #13 Different Spelling of the Same Sound

Read each word aloud. Listen to the sound represented by the bold letter(s). Try to think of other words in which the same sound is spelled in a different way. Write down all the words you think of—the more the better. DON'T LOOK AHEAD AT THE CHART ON PAGE 16 UNLESS YOU'RE REALLY STUCK.

1. m**a**d   2. b**i**t   3. m**e**
4. n**o**   5. lea**f**   6. **sh**oe   7. **t**iger

(Answers are on page 64.)

Some helpful terms

We will have an easier time talking and thinking about spelling if we have some vocabulary to name some special spelling concepts and some symbols to show special usage. We'll give brief definitions here and treat each concept in more detail in the following chapters.

phoneme A phoneme is any single sound. A particular phoneme may have one or more spellings. While italics are used to show words and letters, slash marks like this // are used to enclose sounds. Here's a demonstration of the difference:

> *a* is a word—the English indefinite article.
> /ă/ is the sound in the first syllable of the word *Batman*.

As a reminder, the dictionary used for sounds, symbols, meanings, and pronunciations in this book is *The American Heritage Dictionary of the English Language*. The symbols used in this book for the sounds of words are the symbols used in the first pronunciation entry in that dictionary, unless otherwise noted.

consonant/vowel Consonants and vowels are sounds, not letters. There are, however, letters (for example, *k, l, m, n, x*) that typically spell consonant sounds and letters (*a, e, i, o, u,* and *y*) that typically spell vowel sounds. On occasion, the letters that are sometimes called *consonant letters* are used as auxilliary (helping) letters in spelling a vowel. For example,

> *gh* helps spell the long *i* sound in the word *sigh*.
> *w* helps spell the vowel sound /ow/ in the word *cow*.

Some consonant sounds are spelled using what are sometimes called *vowel letters*.

> *u* spells the /w/ sound in the word *quick*.
> *y* can represent either a vowel sound, as in *happy*, or a consonant sound, as in *yes*.

pronunciation Although some pronunciations are simply "wrong," there is often more than one correct way to say a word. This is because pronunciation of English varies. A teacher may be able to help you identify which differences are because of dialect (the version of English you speak) and which might be caused by mispronunciation.

letter combinations There are two important types of letter combinations:

- **blend** A consonant blend has two distinct sounds that follow one after the other. Some blends are written with two "consonant" letters (for example, *st*) and some have three letters (for example, *str*). All blends include either an *l* (as in *bl*), an *m* (as in *mp*), an *n* (as in *sn*), an *r* (as in *gr*), an *s* (as in *sp*), or a *w* (as in *tw*). Some blends have more than one of these letters.
- **digraph** Literally, the word *digraph* means a string of two letters (*di-* means "two" and *graph* means "letter"). One specialized meaning is "a group of two or three letters that represent a new consonant sound, different from any of the sounds represented by any of the individual letters when used alone."

diphthong A diphthong is a vowel sound that changes during its production. If you say VERY slowly the words *brown, bite,* and *boy,* you will probably hear the vowel sound change at the same time as you feel your mouth move. Each of those words has a vowel diphthong.

How do you spell . . . ?

The charts on the following pages will show you the range of possibilities for spelling some of the main sounds of English. You'll see some patterns that you found when you did Brain Ticklers Set #13 and maybe you'll also see some you didn't think of. You DON'T have to memorize them. You might want to put a sticky note on the first page so you can find it again.

Notes on the charts

- Since people pronounce words differently, some of the words in the chart may appear to you to be in the wrong place. (An * will call your attention to some of these words.) Don't worry about it now.

- _ stands for a choice of "consonant" letters. So, for example, *a_e* could represent *ate, ace, age,* or *ape.*
- A letter combination can appear anywhere in a word, or be an entire word in itself.

> **age**nt (beginning)   dr**ape**r (middle)
> N**ate** (end)   **ace** (whole word)

- **Common** indicates the most frequently occurring spellings of the sound. **Less Common** indicates spellings that are less frequently seen. **Oddball** refers to spellings that are very rare and may even be unique. These are most likely to occur in words that have come into English from another language and retained characteristic spelling patterns from their language of origin. Consult this column only if it is useful to you.
- Letters that are used in a word but either:
  - are not used to make the sounds that they usually make (like *gh* in *sigh*, which you might expect to sound like it does in *cough* or *ghost*)

    or
  - are not obviously needed (like double "consonant" letters), are often called *silent letters.*

    Because they are part of the visual patterns that you have to know to spell words correctly, silent letters are included in the chart, whether or not they are officially part of the spelling of a sound according to language experts. If you are working with a teacher who takes a different approach, you can skip over these examples. You can learn more about silent letters beginning on page 122.
- All words in the chart represent the first pronunciation in *The American Heritage Dictionary* unless there is a note saying *2^(nd)*, which indicates that the second pronunciation is used. Whenever the first and second pronunciations are both included, both are labeled.
- Different dialects of English treat the sounds represented by *American Heritage* as ä, ô, and ŏ very differently. In another major dictionary, ô and ŏ are treated as the same sound. In a third, ä and ŏ are treated as the same. To avoid confusion, these sounds are not included in the chart.

SOUND	SPELLINGS		
Short Vowel Sounds	Common	Less Common	Oddball
short a /ă/	**a** as in *bat*	**a_ _e** as in *trance* **al** as in *half* **au** as in *laugh* **i** as in *meringue*	**a_e** as in *comrade* **ai** as in *plaid*
short e /ĕ/	**e** as in *bet* **ea** as in *bread*	**a** as in *any* **ai** as in *said* **eh** as in *eh*—2nd **ei** as in *leisure* **eo** as in *leopard* **u** as in *bury* **ue** as in *guess*	**ie** as in *friend* **ay** as in *says* **é** as in *créme* **oe** as in *roentgen*
short i /ĭ/	**e** as in *English* **i** as in *bit* **a_e** as in *advantage*	**ia** as in *carriage* **u** as in *busy* **y** as in *abyss*	**i_ _e** as in *grippe* **ie_e** as in *sieve* **o** as in *women* **ui** as in *build* **ee** as in *been*
short u /ŭ/ in an accented syllable	**o** as in *oven* **u** as in *but*	**oo** as in *flood* **ou** as in *trouble*	**e** as in *them*–2nd **o_e** as in *come* **oe** as in *doesn't* **au_e** as in *because* –2nd
schwa /ə/ in an unaccented syllable	**a** as in *balloon* **e** as in *concentration* **o** as in *prison* **u** as in *circus*	**ai** as in *captain* **eo** as in *dungeon* **i** as in *pencil* **ia** as in *special* **iou** as in *anxious* **ou** as in *generous*	**é** as in *protégé* (1st *é*) **eu** as in *chauffeur*–1st
/o͞o/	**o** as in *woman* **u** as in *bull*	**ou** as in *could* **oo** as in *wood*	**oui** as in *bouillon*–2nd

SOUND	SPELLINGS		
Long Vowel Sounds	Common	Less Common	Oddball
long a /ā/	**a** as in *favor* **a_e** as in *male* **a_ _e** as in *paste* **ai** as in *mail* **ai_e** as in *praise* **ay** as in *may*	**ae** as in *Gaelic* **au_e** as in *gauge* **é** as in *soufflé* **ée** as in *née* **e_e** as in *crepe or crêpe* **ea** as in *great* **ee** as in *matinee* **ei** as in *veil* **eig** as in *deign* **eigh** as in *neighbor* **ey** as in *prey* **(u)et** as in *bouquet*	**aig** as in *arraign* **aigh** as in *straight* **ao** as in *gaol* **aye** as in *aye* (always) **e** as in *rodeo*–2nd **eh** as in *eh*–1st **oeh** as in *foehn*–2nd **(u)ay** as in *quay*–2nd
long e /ē/	**e** as in *me* **e_e** as in *gene* **ea** as in *peal* **ee** as in *peek* **y** as in *happy*	**ae** as in *archaeology* **ea_e** as in *peace* **ei_e** as in *receive* **ie** as in *thief* **ie_e** as in *believe* **ey** as in *key* **i** as in *curious* **i_e** as in *machine* **is** as in *chassis* **oe** as in *phoenix* **(u)y** as in *soliloquy*	**a** as in *bologna* **eo** as in *people* **(u)ay** as in *quay*–1st
long i /ī/	**i** as in *mild* **i_e** as in *mile* **ie** as in *lie* **igh** as in *might* **y** as in *my*	**ai** as in *Thailand* **ay** as in *papaya* **ei** as in *stein* **eigh** as in *height* **eye** as in *eye* **ia** as in *vial*–2nd **ig** as in *sign* **is** as in *island* **uy** as in *buy* **ye** as in *bye* **y_e** as in *rhyme*	**ai_ _e** as in *faille* **ais** as in *aisle* **aye** as in *aye* (yea) **oy** as in *coyote* **ui_e** as in *guide* **uye** as in *guyed*
long o /ō/	**o** as in *no* **o_e** as in *mole* **oa** as in *moat* **oe** as in *doe* **ow** as in *mow*	**au** as in *chauvinist* **eau** as in *plateau* **oh** as in *oh* **ol** as in *folk* **ou** as in *soul* **ough** as in *though* **owe** as in *owe*	**aoh** as in *pharaoh* **aux** as in *faux* **eo** as in *yeoman* **eou** as in *Seoul* **ew** as in *sew* **ho** as in *mho* **ô_e** as in *côte* **oo** as in *brooch* **ot** as in *tarot*
long u /ōō/	**ew** as in *stew* **o** as in *to* **oo** as in *soon* **o_e** as in *whose* **u** as in *Ruth* **u_e** as in *June*	**eu** as in *sleuth* **oe** as in *canoe* **ou** as in *you* **ue** as in *blue* **ui** as in *suit*	**ieu** as in *adieu*–2nd **ough** as in *through* **oup** as in *coup* **ou_e** as in *coupe* **ou_ _e** as in *mousse* **ougha** as in *brougham* **wo** as in *two*
long u with y in front /yōō/	**ew** as in *fewer* **u** as in *human* **ue** as in *barbecue* **u_e** as in *mule*	**eu** as in *feud* **iew** as in *view* **you** as in *youth*	**eau** as in *beauty* **ieu** as in *adieu* **u_ _e** as in *butte* **ueue** as in *queue*

SOUND	SPELLINGS		
Vowel Sounds	**Common**	**Less Common**	**Oddball**
/oi/	**oi** as in *boil* **oy** as in *boy*		**oig** as in *coign* **uoi** as in *quoin* **uoy** as in *buoy*
/ou/	**ou** as in *cloud* **ow** as in *frown*	**hou** as in *hour* **ough** as in *bough*	**ao** as in *Tao* **aue** as in *sauerbraten* **iao** as in *ciao*
/âr/	**air** as in *lair* **ar** as in *parent* **are** as in *snare* **ear** as in *pear*	**aer** as in *aerobic* **aire** as in *millionaire* **er** as in *scherzo* **eyr** as in *eyrie*	**ayer** as in *prayer* (not the person, who's a /prā ər/) **e'er** as in *e'er* **ere** as in *ere* **eyre** as in *eyre* **heir** as in *heir* **iere** as in *premiere*–2nd **uar** as in *guarantee*
/îr/	**ear** as in *dear* **eer** as in *deer* **er** as in *zero* **ere** as in *here*	**eir** as in *weird* **ier** as in *tier*	**aer** as in *aerie*–2nd **eor** as in *theory* **eyr** as in *eyrie*–2nd **iere** as in *premiere*–1st **ière** as in *première* **yr** as in *Tyr*
/ôr/	**ar** as in *quarrel* **or** as in *condor* **ore** as in *galore*	**aur** as in *centaur* **oar** as in *roar* **oor** as in *door* **our** as in *four*	**awr** as in *Lawrence* **oer** as in *Boer*–2nd **orr** as in *torr*
/ûr/	**er** as in *kernel* **eur** as in *chauffeur*–2nd **ir** as in *bird* **ur** as in *burn*	**ear** as in *learn* **urr** as in *burr* **yr** as in *myrtle*	**ere** as in *were* **irr** as in *whirr* **olo** as in *colonel* **or** as in *work* **our** as in *courtesy* **yrrh** as in *myrrh*

SOUND	SPELLINGS		
Consonant Sounds	Common	Less Common	Oddball
/ch/	**ch** as in *chimp* **tch** as in *watch*	**c(e)** as in *cello* **t(e)** as in *righteous* **t(i)** as in *question* **t(ure)** as in *creature*	**cz** as in *Czech*
/f/	**f** as in *leaf* **ph** as in *photo*	**ff** as in *difficult* **ft** as in *often* **gh** as in *tough* **lf** as in *calf*	
/g/	**g** as in *girl* **gg** as in *egg*	**gh** as in *ghost* **gue** as in *dialogue* **x** as in *exam*	
/h/	**h** as in *human*	**g** as in *Gila monster* **j** as in *junta* **wh** as in *who*	
/j/	**dg(e)** as in *judge* **g(e)** as in *gentle* **j** as in *jump*	**dg(i)** as in *lodging* **g(i)** as in *giraffe* **d(u)** as in *graduate*	**d(i)** as in *soldier* **dj(e)** as in *adjective* **g(a)** as in *gaol* **gg(e)** as in *exaggerate*
/k/	**c** as in *camel* **ck** as in *back* **k** as in *kangaroo* **q(u)** as in *conquer*	**cc** as in *accurate* **ch** as in *ache* **cq(u)** as in *lacquer* **kh** as in *khaki* **lk** as in *walk* **que** as in *oblique*	**cch** as in *saccharine* **kk** as in *trekked* **q** as in *FAQ* **q(i)** as in *Iraqi* **x** as in *exceed*
/l/	**l** as in *late* **ll** as in *troll*	**sl** as in *isle*	**lh** as in *lhasa apso* **ln** as in *kiln–2nd*

SOUND	SPELLINGS		
Consonant Sounds	Common	Less Common	Oddball
/m/	**m** as in *mom* **mm** as in *mommy*	**gm** as in *diaphragm* **lm** as in *calm* **mb** as in *lamb* **mn** as in *limn*	**chm** as in *drachm*
/n/	**n** as in *pin* **nn** as in *inn*	**gn** as in *gnat* **kn** as in *knee* **mn** as in *mnemonic* **nd** as in *handsome* **pn** as in *pneumonia*	**dn** as in *Wednesday*
/ng/	**ng** as in *strong* **nk** as in *think*	**ngue** as in *tongue*	**ngg** as in *mahjongg* **nx** as in *anxiety*
/p/	**p** as in *pig* **pp** as in *guppy*	**ph** as in *shepherd*	**gh** as in *hiccough*
/r/	**r** as in *rare*	**rh** as in *rhythm* **rr** as in *terror* **rrh** as in *cirrhosis* **wr** as in *wring*	**rt** as in *mortgage* **l(o)** as in *colonel*
/s/	**c(e)** as in *celery* **c(i)** as in *city* **c(y)** as in *fancy* **s** as in *slime* **ss** as in *brass*	**ps** as in *pseudonym* **sc** as in *science* **st** as in *listen* **sw** as in *sword* **z** as in *quartz*	**sch** as in *schism*–2nd **sth** as in *isthmus*
/sh/	**c(i)** as in *suspicion* **sh** as in *shoe* **s(i)** as in *vision* **ss(i)** as in *mission* **t(i)** as in *gumption*	**c(e)** as in *oceanic* **ch** as in *chandelier* **s(u)** as in *sugar* **sch(i)** as in *schism* **sc(i)** as in *conscience* **s(e)** as in *nauseous* **ss(u)** as in *tissue*	**che** as in *cache* **chs(i)** as in *fuchsia* **psh** as in *pshaw* **zh** as in *pirozhki*
/t/	**t** as in *tiger* **tt** as in *cattle*	**bt** as in *debt* **ed** as in *vanished* **pt** as in *pterodactyl* **th** as in *thyme*	**cht** as in *yacht* **ct** as in *indict*

SOUND	SPELLINGS		
Consonant Sounds	**Common**	**Less Common**	**Oddball**
/v/	**v** as in *van*	**f** as in *of* **lv(e)** as in *calve*	
/w/	**(q)u** as in *quality* **w** as in *wet* **wh** as in *who*	**(g)u** as in *language* **o** as in *once* **(s)u** as in *suave* **ui** as in *cuisine*	
/y/	**y** as in *yum*	**i** as in *alleluia*	**j** as in *hallelujah*
/z/	**z** as in *zebra*	**s** as in *his* **s(e)** as in *turquoise* **ss** as in *scissors* **x** as in *xylophone* **zz** as in *buzz*	**cz** as in *czar* **thes** as in *clothes* **ts** as in *tsar*
/zh/	**s(i)** as in *decision* **s(u)** as in *unusual*	**g(e)** as in *garage* **z(u)** as in *azure*	**g(i)** as in *regime* **t(i)** as in *equation*

BRAIN TICKLERS
Set #14 Origins of Different Spellings

1. Choose 20 different spellings from the chart. Look up each of the example words in the dictionary to find out what language it came from originally. What conclusions can you draw?

2. Look up the original languages for all the example words for one sound that has at least six spellings. What conclusions can you draw?

(Answers are on page 64.)

The sound/sight strategy: SSS

Here's an overview of one strategy that can help you a lot. Let's call it the **sound/sight strategy** or **SSS**:

1. Look for visual patterns.

2. Look for sound patterns.

3. See how the sound patterns correspond to the visual patterns.

4. See if you can find a rule or rules that explains the relationship between the sound and the visual pattern.

5. Look for more examples that support the rule.

6. Check your rule or rules for exceptions.

Here's a model for you using the words *bread, greed, head, leaf, neat,* and *seed.* Examining the list, I see two visual and two sound patterns.

VISUAL PATTERNS		SOUND PATTERNS	
ea	**ee**	**/ē/**	**/ĕ/**
bread	greed	greed	bread
head	seed	leaf	head
leaf		neat	
neat		seed	

But it is only by looking at both visual AND sound patterns together that we can see what's really going on: **three** patterns:

SSS RESULTS		
/ē/		**/ĕ/**
ea	ee	ea
leaf/neat	greed/seed	bread/head

BRAIN TICKLERS
Set #15 Practice the Sight/Sound Strategy

Extend the patterns of /ē/ and /ĕ/ by adding four words of your own choosing to each of the three categories in the chart.

/ē/		/ĕ/
ea	**ee**	**ea**
leaf	greed	bread
neat	seed	head

(Answers are on page 65.)

ENGLISH SPELLING PATTERNS OVERVIEW

Earlier in this chapter, you saw that some sounds in English can be represented by quite a few different letters and letter combinations. The chart you saw beginning on page 49 looked at spelling from a sound point of view. Now, we're going to switch to a visual vantage point and look at the letter combinations to see which different sounds they can spell.

Some letter combinations for vowel sounds

The letters that most often spell vowel sounds (*a, e, i, o, u, y*), which are sometimes called "the vowels," can be used either alone or in certain combinations, like *ea, oo,* or *ie.* Other combinations, like *iy* or *io,* are rarely, if ever seen. One of the biggest challenges that many find with spelling English words, is that both the letters *a, e, i, o, u,* and *y,* whether alone or in the customary combinations, can spell more than one sound.

Identical twins

Do you know any sets of identical twins? Have you ever called one of them by the wrong name? Chances are that if you did, you didn't get the answer you expected. Look below, and you'll see a set of what we might call identical quintuplets: they look the same, but they're actually different.

1. *i* spells /ă/ in *meringue*

2. *i* spells /ĭ/ in *bit*

3. *i* spells /ə/ in *pencil*

4. *i* spells /ē/ in *curious*

5. *i* spells /ī/ in *mild*

Now, what happens if you call one of them by the name belonging to another of them? In most cases, you just get a strange pronunciation of a word. But if you call *i* No. 2 by *i* No. 1's name, you know what happens? You hear the word *bat* instead of the word *bit.* And if you call *i* No. 2 by *i* No. 3's name, you hear the word *but* instead of the word *bit.* If you call *i* No. 2 by *i* No. 4's name, you hear *beat* or *beet* instead of *bit.* And if you call *i* No. 2 by *i* No. 5's name, you hear *bite* instead of *bit.* Whoops!

BRAIN TICKLERS
Set #16 Letters That Spell Multiple Sounds

Use the chart on pages 15–21. For each letter or set of letters, write down the different sounds it can spell. Use the slashes and the symbols from the chart, plus a sample word. The sample word can be from the chart, or you can choose one of your own. If you're not sure, check it in a dictionary. A sample is given for you.

Letter(s)	Sound Symbol	Sample Word
a	/ă/	fabulous
a		
e		
i		
o		
u		
y		
ai		
au		
ea		
ei		
ie		
oo		
ou		
ow		
ui		
ear		

(Answers are on page 65.)

BRAIN TICKLERS
Set #17 Analyze a Spelling Rule

There's a saying used in teaching spelling: "When two vowels go walking, the first one does the talking." Analyze the chart you made in Brain Tickler Set #15. Find examples that support the saying. Find examples that don't support it. What conclusions can you draw?

(Answers are on page 67.)

Some letter combinations for consonant sounds

Party time

Have you ever been in this situation: You want to get together with two or three of your good friends, but they don't know each other, and you're not sure what will happen when they're together. Maybe they'll all try to assert themselves, and you'll feel like you're just a bunch of individuals, not a group. Maybe one will do all the talking, and the others will be silent. Or maybe you'll have a wonderful mixture in which every person contributes—a totally new experience. Any of these three things can happen when you combine more than one "consonant" letter.

Three possibilities

When we put consonant letters together, three things can happen.

1. The "consonant" letters all keep "talking," and we get a **blend** in which each individual letter's sound can be heard.

"Consonant" letter combinations that make blends:

BLENDS			
INITIAL BLEND			**FINAL BLEND**
bl as in *blue*	**fr** as in *fro*	**sp** as in *spun*	**ft** as in *heft*
cl as in *clue*	**gr** as in *grow*	**spr** as in *sprung*	**ld** as in *held*
fl as in *flu*	**pr** as in *prow*	**st** as in *stun*	**lt** as in *halt*
gl as in *glue*	**tr** as in *trowel*	**str** as in *straw*	**mp** as in *damp*
pl as in *plow*	**sc** as in *scan*	**sw** as in *swung*	**nd** as in *sand*
sl as in *slow*	**scr** as in *scram*	**tw** as in *twig*	**nt** as in *sent*
br as in *brow*	**sk** as in *skill*	**wh** as in *Whig*	**sk** as in *task*
cr as in *crow*	**sm** as in *smug*		**sp** as in *clasp*
dr as in *drop*	**sn** as in *snug*		**st** as in *test*

2. At least one of the "consonant" letters is not heard (a **silent partner**). This can happen either when the consonant letters are the same or when different letters are included in the combination. Asterisks mark less frequent combinations.

Consonant letter combinations with a silent partner:

SILENT PARTNERS			
Double Letters	**Letter Combinations**		
bb as in *hobby*	**bt** as in *debt**	**kn** as in *knee*	**pt** as in *pterodactyl*
cc as in *acclaim* (not access)	**cch** as in *saccharine**	**lh** as in *lhasa apso*	**rh** as in *rhythm*
dd as in *daddy*	**chm** as in *drachm**	**lk** as in *walk*	**rrh** as in *cirrhosis*
ff as in *taffy*	**cht** as in *yacht**	**lm** as in *calm*	**rt** as in *mortgage**
gg as in *baggy*	**ct** as in *indict**	**ln** as in *kiln*–2nd	**sc** as in *science*
kk as in *trekked**	**ck** as in *clock*	**lv(e)** as in *calve*	**sch** as in *schism**–2nd
ll as in *hilly*	**dg(e)** as in *judge*	**mb** as in *lamb*	**st** as in *listen**
mm as in *yummy*	**dg(i)** as in *lodging*	**mn** as in *mnemonic* /n/	**sth** as in *isthmus**
nn as in *bunny*	**dn** as in *Wednesday**	**mn** as in *limn* /m/	**sw** as in *sword*
pp as in *happy*	**ft** as in *often*	**nd** as in *handsome**	**tch** as in *watch*
rr as in *hurry*	**gh** as in *ghost*	**ph** as in *shepherd*	**th** as in *thyme*
ss as in *sissy*	**gm** as in *diaphragm**	**pn** as in *pneumonia*	**ts** as in *tsar*
tt as in *chatty*	**gn** as in *gnaw*	**ps** as in *pseudonym*	**wh** as in *who*
vv as in *savvy*	**kh** as in *khaki**	**psh** as in *pshaw**	**wr** as in *wring*
zz as in *fizzy*			

3. The consonant letter combination makes a new sound that neither can make alone (**digraph**).

Consonant letter combinations with a new sound (digraphs):

DIGRAPHS	
ch as in ***chimp*** /ch/	**sh** as in ***shoe*** /sh/
cz as in ***Czech*** /ch/	**tch** as in ***watch*** (digraph with silent partner) /ch/
gh as in *hiccough* /p/	**th** (voiced) as in ***than*** /th/
ng as in *strong* /ng/	**th** (unvoiced) as in ***thanks*** /th/
ph as in ***photo*** /f/	

Voiced and *unvoiced* have specialized meanings here. They refer to a distinction in the way a sound is produced. When you pronounce voiced sounds, your vocal chords vibrate. When you pronounce unvoiced sounds, they don't. Put your fingers gently on the front of your throat and say the following pairs of sounds, and you'll feel it:

Voiced Sounds	Unvoiced Sounds
/z/	/s/
/g/	/k/
/v/	/f/
/d/	/t/
/b/	/p/
/j/	/ch/

Now try saying *the* (voiced) and *thread* (unvoiced). Do you hear and feel the difference?

BRAIN TICKLERS
Set #18 Blends, Digraphs, and Silent Partners

1. Write five words that contain a blend and are not in the blend chart.

2. Write five words that contain a silent partner and are not in the silent partner chart.

3. Write five words that contain a consonant digraph that are not in the digraph chart.

(Answers are on page 67.)

BRAIN TICKLERS—THE ANSWERS

Set #11 page 43

Answers will vary depending on choice of word and spellings. One possible response is:

Oklahoma spelled Auquelliouhoughmmi. Explanation:

au as in *chauvinist*	**iou** as in *anxious*	**mm** as in *Mommy*
que as in *oblique*	**h** as in *hamburger*	**i** as in *pencil*
ll as in *llama*	**ough** as in *though*	

Set #12 page 44

1. Possible response: An alphabet that related sounds to symbols could potentially make it easier to spell. I think that it would really be difficult to switch alphabets for several reasons. First, it would be hard to learn, with more than twice the symbols of our existing alphabet. Second, there's so much already written in our existing alphabet, that it would be very difficult to make the switch.

2. It says, "Chapter Two: Overview of English Spelling."

Set #13, page 45

The words will vary. Possible responses include:
1. m**a**d   comrade, salve, laugh
2. b**i**t   marriage, business, guilty, gym
3. m**e**   meal, sneeze, treat, peat, Pete, ski, marine, receive, grieve, silly
4. n**o**   beau, stole, soap, toe, flow
5. lea**f**   scaffold, photograph, trough
6. **sh**oe   ocean, chamois, vision, mission, nation, sugar
7. **t**iger   rattle, Ptolemy, flashed, Thai, debtor, yacht, indict

Set #14, page 54

1. Answers will vary. Possible responses include:

azure Persian   **knee** Old English   **slime** Old English
bouquet Old French   **meringue** French   **soufflé** Latin
buzz Middle English   **pneumonia** Greek   **sword** Old English
camel Semitic   **rhyme** Greek   **thyme** Greek
chandelier Latin   **rhythm** Greek   **women** Old English
fuchsia New Latin   **schism** Greek   **yacht** Middle German
garage Frankish   **science** Latin

Possible conclusion: From this sampling, the English language seems to have "inherited" many words from Greek, Old English, and Latin, and some (but fewer) from Persian, Frankish, French, Semitic, and German.

2. Possible response: /zh/

Word	Language of Origin
decision	Latin
unusual	Latin
garage	Frankish
azure	Persian
regime	Latin
equation	Latin

Set #15, page 56

Possible responses:

Long *e* /ē/ spelled ea: heat, beat, seat, treat, sheaf, read (present tense), team, scream, dream, cheat

Long *e* /ē/ spelled ee: greet, feed, speed, need, heed, freed, parakeet, sleet, seem, skeet, creed

Short *e* /ĕ/ spelled ea: thread, tread, dead, read (past tense), lead (the metal), ahead, dread

Set #16, page 58

Letter(s)	Sound Symbol	Sample Word
a	/ă/ /ĕ/ /ĭ/ /ə/ /ā/ /ē/	bat any portage balloon favor bologna
e	/ĕ/ /ĭ/ /ŭ/ /ə/ /ā/ /ē/	bet English them concentration rodeo–2nd me
i	/ă/ /ĭ/ /ə/ /ē/ /ī/	meringue bit pencil curious mild
o	/ĭ/ /ŭ/ /ə/ / o͝o / /ō/ / o͞o /	women done prison woman no to

Letter(s)	Sound Symbol	Sample Word
u	/ĕ/	bury
	/ĭ/	busy
	/ŭ/	but
	/ə/	circus
	/ŏŏ/	bull
	/ōō/	Ruth
	/yōō/	human
y	/ĭ/	abyss
	/ē/	happy
	/ī/	my
ai	/ă/	plaid
	/ĕ/	said
	/ə/	captain
	/ā/	mail
	/ī/	Thailand
au	/ă/	laugh
	/ō/	chauvinist
ea	/ĕ/	bread
	/ā/	great
	/ē/	peal
ei	/ĕ/	leisure
	/ā/	veil
	/ē/	receive
	/ī/	stein
ie	/ĕ/	friend
	/ē/	thief
	/ī/	lie
oo	/ŭ/	flood
	/ŏŏ/	wood
	/ō/	brooch
	/ōō/	soon
ou	/u/	trouble
	/ə/	generous
	/ŏŏ/	could
	/ō/	soul
	/ōō/	you
	/ou/	cloud

Letter(s)	Sound Symbol	Sample Word
ow	/ō/ /ou/	m**ow** fro**w**n
ui	/ĭ/ /o͞o/	b**ui**ld s**ui**t
ear	/âr/ /ûr/ /îr/	p**ear** l**ear**n d**ear**

Set #17, page 59

It's true when *ai* spells /ā/; when *ea* spells /ĕ/ or /ē/; when *ei* spells /ē/; when *ie* spells /ī/; when *ow* spells /ō/; and when *ui* spells /o͞o/. In all other cases it is not true. You may conclude that it has limited use and that it might be more confusing than helpful.

Set #18, page 63

Answers will vary. Possible responses:

1.

BLENDS			
Initial			**Final**
bl as in *blossom*	**fr** as in *frontier*	**sp** as in *spit*	**ft** as in *left*
cl as in *clean*	**gr** as in *granola*	**spr** as in *spring*	**ld** as in *shield*
fl as in *flood*	**pr** as in *prune*	**st** as in *statue*	**lt** as in *salt*
gl as in *glade*	**tr** as in *trigonometry*	**str** as in *stream*	**mp** as in *damp*
pl as in *plaid*	**sc** as in *scamp*	**sw** as in *swift*	**nd** as in *kind*
sl as in *sleigh*	**scr** as in *scream*	**tw** as in *twilight*	**nt** as in *dent*
br as in *breakfast*	**sk** as in *skim*	**wh** as in *whale*	**sk** as in *ask*
cr as in *creep*	**sm** as in *smelly*		**st** as in *last*
dr as in *dragon*	**sn** as in *snare drum*		

2.

SILENT PARTNERS	
Double Letters	**Letter Combinations**

Double Letters		Letter Combinations	
bb as in *babble*	**mm** as in *hammer*	**dg(e)** as in *judge*	**ps** as in *psalm*
cc as in *raccoon*	**nn** as in *penny*	**ft** as in *soften*	**pt** as in *ptarmigan*
dd as in *waddle*	**pp** as in *sloppy*	**ght** as in *night*	**rh** as in *rhapsody*
ff as in *giraffe*	**rr** as in *ferry*	**gn** as in *gnarled*	**sc** as in *scenic*
gg as in *giggle*	**ss** as in *hiss*	**kn** as in *knight*	**st** as in *fasten*
kk as in *bookkeeper*	**tt** as in *cattle*	**lk** as in *chalk*	**tch** as in *latch*
ll as in *wall*	**zz** as in *fuzzy*	**lm** as in *balmy*	**wh** as in *when*–2ⁿᵈ
		mb as in *plumber*	**wr** as in *wrong*
		pn as in *pneumatic*	

3.

CONSONANT DIGRAPHS	
ch as in *charm* /ch/	**tch** as in *latch* (digraph with silent partner) /ch/
ng as in *sing* /ng/	**th** (voiced) as in *that* /th/
ph as in *phonograph* /f/	**th** (unvoiced) as in *thumb* /th/
sh as in *sheep* /sh/	

Did you know that the letters *wh* beginning a word are pronounced /hw/ in many dialects? In fact, some words that begin *w-h* used to begin with the spelling h-w! *Whelp* used to be *hwelp*. *While* used to be *hwil*. Hwat do you think of that?

CHAPTER THREE

"Let's Start at the Very Beginning"

THREE-LETTER WORDS: "A VERY GOOD PLACE TO START"

Do you remember kindergarten and first grade? Often in early schooling, simple facts in mathematics and spelling are taught with the idea of family. There are number families like 2, 5, and 7 that you can put together in addition and subtraction problems. There are word families, too.

To begin with, there are some really popular patterns of "consonant" and "vowel" letters. To show them, we use a capital *V* to represent a "vowel" letter and a capital *C* to represent a "consonant" letter.

In the area of three-letter words, we can find CCV words like *pry*, and VCC words like *ohm*. There are CVV words like *goo*, VVC words like *aah*, and VCV words like *axe*. Just for review, we're going to spend a little time with three-letter word families that fit the most common pattern: CVC.

The kiddle in the middle

Having just three letters in a CVC word certainly narrows the possibilities for letter combinations. For example, no blends or diagraphs are possible. But there's more! Can you think of ANY three letter CVC words that have a *y* in the middle? No? Well, there are at least two words—*gyp* and *gym*—but not many, so the possibilities for letter combinations just got even fewer. There just aren't that many things you can do with only three letters. But what you CAN do is worth exploring.

Group 1—The rhyming group

First, let's define one group of three-letter words and then hunt for families that fit.

> Group 1 is a collection of three-letter words that have the same middle letter and the same final letter. Most of the words in each family of this group rhyme with each other.

An example of a family in this group is: *bun, fun, gun, Hun* (as in Attila), *nun, pun, run, sun.*

Notice how the list goes in alphabetical order? The easiest way to find members of a family is to go through the alphabet and try each letter on the front of the word to see if it fits. Also notice that proper nouns are allowed into the family. So are weird words. If you're doing the *it* family, you can include *zit.* Is there a family for *ez?* You bet. *Pez* (those little candies) and *fez* (a felt hat worn in eastern Mediterranean countries) will make a family for *ez,* if anyone asks you. The only rule is, if you're working with others, don't include any words that would offend them or show disrespect.

Can you think of any two three-letter words that have the same two last letters, but do NOT rhyme?

HINT: If this happens, it's usually because the vowel sound in the two words is different.

How about *cut* and *put?*

BRAIN TICKLERS
Set #19 Three-Letter Words—Rhyming Group

So who has the biggest family in Group 1? I'll give you a hint: families like *ez* are minuscule (really small) compared with some families you can find. So here's a challenge: What's the biggest family you can find in Group 1? On your mark, get set, go! Hint: If you aren't sure whether the letters you've put together make a word, check the biggest dictionary you can find. (The bigger the dictionary, the more words are in it—and yours might be there, too!)

(Answers are on page 84.)

Group 2—New beginnings

Are you ready for the next group? This group of words all begin with the same letters, but end with a different letter.

Group 2 is a collection of three-letter words that have the same initial letter and the same middle letter.

An example of a family in this group is: *bad, bag, bah, bam, ban, bar, bat, bay.*

BRAIN TICKLERS
Set #20 Three-Letter Words — Same Beginning

This may be harder to do, but give it a whirl—
what's the largest family you can find for
Group 2?

(Answers are on page 85.)

Family trees

In all your years of using the English language, you've probably
learned some things about English that you don't even realize.
See if these conclusions match your experiences in this chapter:

1. The letters x, q, y, c, and z are like distant cousins eight times
   removed—you hardly ever see them in English words, period,
   let alone three-letter words. Can you add other letters to this
   list?

2. The letter u is like an uncle who lives a few hours away—he
   appears only when he happens to be in town, less often than
   a, e, i, and o.

MORE ABOUT CONSONANT LETTER BLENDS AND DIGRAPHS

Initial digraphs and blends: The musketeers and the molecules

Imagine a CVC word with one or two extra consonant letters in front of it. Now you've got a CCVC word or a CCCVC word. The two or three consonant letters at the beginning of these words can fit into three different categories that we already met on page 71.

1. They can form a **blend,** in which you hear the sound of each letter one right after the other, like the first two letters of *blend: bl.*

    A blend is like the Three Musketeers: each one of them has his identity as a musketeer, and yet, when you see them together, you're still aware of their individual personalities. Try saying these blends to yourself: *st, tw, nd, cr.*

2. Or they can form a **digraph,** a term which, you may remember, we're using to refer to any group of two or three "consonant" letters representing a sound that is NOT the same as the sound of any of the individual letters alone. Examples are *sh, th, ch.*

   A digraph is like a molecule. When you put oxygen and hydrogen together, you get water, and its properties are different than the properties of either component. By joining them together, you have made something new and different.

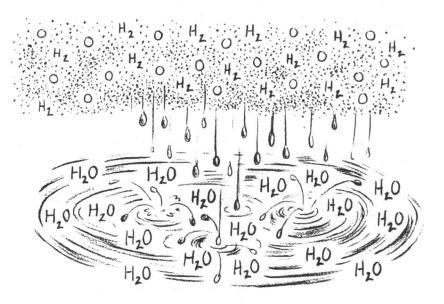

3. They can also be a letter set with one or more silent partners. We'll learn more about those beginning on page 122. For the rest of this chapter, we'll focus on blends and digraphs.

BRAIN TICKLERS
Set #21 Initial Blends and Digraphs

Here is a collection of initial consonant blends and digraphs.

bl	fl	pr	sm	sw
br	fr	sc	sn	th
ch	gl	sh	sp	tr
cl	gr	scr	spr	tw
cr	ph	sk	st	wh
dr	pl	sl	str	

1. Say them aloud to decide which are which. Sort them into a group of blends and a group of digraphs.

2. Okay, now take the same list and sort it into some other groups that you think are useful. Explain in a sentence or two how you formed your groupings.

(Answers are on page 86.)

BRAIN TICKLERS
Set #22 Molecule Words

Read each list of words below. What do the words in each list have in common? They all are "molecule" words, and they all start with the same two letters. Sort each list into categories that make sense to you. Write a sentence or two explaining why you grouped the items the way you did. Then add three words to each category you made.

1. chalet   cheese   chicken
    chameleon   chef   chimpanzee
    Charlotte   chemist   choir
    chauffeur   cherry   cholesterol

2. thank-you   these   though
    thaw   they   thunder
    the   thief
    then   thistle

(Answers are on page 86.)

BRAIN TICKLERS
Set #23 Musketeer Words

Here are some "musketeers": Make a list of five words that begin with each initial consonant blend listed below.

bl	fl	pr	sm	str
br	fr	sc	sn	sw
cl	gl	scr	sp	tr
cr	gr	sk	spr	tw
dr	pl	sl	st	wh

(Answers are on page 87.)

BRAIN TICKLERS
Set #24 Analyze Initial Consonant Groups

Using what you've learned so far, explain the group of initial consonant letters in each of the following words.

thrice   phrase   shrapnel   chrome

(Answers are on page 87.)

Final digraphs and blends: More musketeers and molecules

Imagine a CVC word with one or two extra consonant letters following it. Now you've got a CVCC word or a CVCCC word. The two or three "consonant" letters at the end can fit into the same two categories: blends ("musketeers") or digraphs ("molecules").

BRAIN TICKLERS
Set #25 Initial Blends and Digraphs That Can Be Final

Take a look at this list of initial blends and digraphs. See if you can figure out which ones can also be final blends and digraphs. Make a list and write down a word for each one that works as an ending.

bl	fl	pr	sm	sw
br	fr	sc	sn	th
ch	gl	sh	sp	tr
cl	gr	scr	spr	tw
cr	ph	sk	st	wh
dr	pl	sl	str	

(Answers are on page 87.)

BRAIN TICKLERS
Set #26 Brainstorm Final Blends

Now, using your memory (and a dictionary), try to think of some blends and digraphs that we haven't covered yet but that can appear at the end of words.

(Answers are on page 88.)

BRAIN TICKLERS
Set #27 Sort Final Blends and Digraphs

Take this list of final blends and digraphs and sort it into groups that you think are useful. Explain in a sentence or two how you formed your groupings.

ch	mp	ph	sk	th
ft	nd	rd	sp	ts
ld	ng	sc	st	tz
lt	nt	sh	tch	

(Answers are on page 88.)

BRAIN TICKLERS
Set #28 TCH and CH Words

The digraphs *tch* and *ch* both spell the sound /ch/ at the end of a word. Make a list of as many *tch* and *ch* words as you can think of. What patterns do you find in the middle of your words? Sort the list, not by the final digraph, but by the LETTERS BETWEEN the final digraph and the initial consonant letter, blend, or digraph (if there is one—if not, start with the vowel or two adjacent vowels closest to the final blend or digraph). Write a sentence or two explaining how you grouped the words.

(Answers are on page 88.)

BRAIN TICKLERS
Set #29 Identity Words That End with Particular Blends and Digraphs

Now, for each final blend and digraph listed below, write five words that use that ending.

ft	nd	ph	sk	th
ld	ng	rd	sp	ts
lt	nk	sh	st	tz
mp	nt			

(Answers are on page 88.)

BRAIN TICKLERS
Set #30 Analyze Final Consonant Groups

Using what you've learned, explain the groups of final consonant letters in the following words. What kinds of groups are they?

depth   search   hearts   tenth   harsh

(Answers are on page 89.)

BRAIN TICKLERS—THE ANSWERS

Set #19, page 74

Possible responses:

Some of the larger families of Group 1 include:

ED family	bed, fed, Jed, led, Ned, red, Ted, wed, zed (another name for the letter *z*) (9)
EW family	dew, few, hew, Jew, mew, new, pew, sew, yew (9)
OD family	cod, God, hod (holder for coal), mod, nod, pod, rod, sod (grass), Tod (9)
OP family	bop, cop, fop, hop, lop, mop, pop, sop, top (9)
UG family	bug, dug, hug, jug, lug, mug, pug, rug, tug (9)
AR family	bar, car, far, gar (a fish), jar, Lar (a Roman household god), mar, par, tar, war (10)
AT family	bat, cat, fat, hat, mat, pat, rat, sat, tat, vat (10)
IN family	bin, din, fin, gin, kin, pin, sin, tin, win, yin (Chinese: female cosmic principle, opposite of yang) (10)

IT family	bit, fit, git (British for a worthless person), hit, kit, lit, pit, sit, wit, zit (10)
OG family	bog, cog, dog, fog, hog, jog, log, nog (as in eggnog), pog (paper bottlecaps), tog (dress up) (10)
AN family	ban, can, Dan, fan, man, Nan, pan, ran, tan, van, wan (11)
AP family	cap, gap, lap, map, nap, pap, rap, sap, tap, yap, zap (11)
ET family	bet, get, jet, let, met, net, pet, set, vet, wet, yet (11)
OT family	cot, dot, got, hot, jot, lot, not, pot, rot, sot, tot, wot (British verb meaning "know") (12)
AD family	bad, cad, dad, fad, gad, had, lad, mad, pad, rad (a unit of radiation), sad, tad, wad (13)
EN family	Ben, den, fen (low land covered with water), hen, Jen, Ken, men, pen, sen (an Asian coin), ten, yen, wen (a cyst), Zen (13)
OW family	bow, cow, Dow (Jones average), how, low, mow, now, pow, row, sow, tow, vow, wow, yow (14)

Set #20, page 75

Possible responses:

PE family	ped, peg, pen, pep, per, pet, pew, Pez (8)
SA family	sad, sag, Sam, sap, sat, saw, sax, say (8)
SI family	sic, Sid, sin, sip, sir, Sis, sit, six (8)
SO family	sob, sod, Sol, son, sop, sot, sow, soy (8)
TA family	tab, tad, tag, tan, tap, tar, tat, tax (8)
CA family	cab, cad, Cal, can, cap, car, cat, caw, cay (a coral reef) (9)
MA family	Mac, mad, man, map, mar, mat, maw, Max, may (9)
PA family	pad, pal, Pam, pan, par, pat, paw, pax, pay (9)
WA family	WAC (Women's Army Corps), wad, WAF (Women in the Air Force), wag, wan, war, was, wax, way (9)
RA family	rad (dose of radiation), rag, rah, Raj (British rule in India), ram, ran, rap, rat, raw, ray (10)

Set #21, page 78

Possible responses:

1. **Blends:** *bl br cl cr dr fl fr gl gr pl pr sc scr sk sl sm sn sp spr st str sw tr tw wh*
   Digraphs: *ch ph sh th*

2. Answers may vary. Possible responses:

three-letter blends:	*scr, spr, str*
blends with a /k/ sound:	*cl, cr, sc, scr, sk*
l-blends:	*bl, cl, fl, gl, pl, sl*
p-blends:	*pl, pr, spr*
r-blends:	*br, cr, dr, fr, gr, pr, scr, spr, str, tr*
s-blends:	*sc, scr, sk, sl, sm, sn, sp, spr, st, str, sw*
t-blends:	*st, str, tr, tw*
digraphs:	*ch, ph, sh, th, wh*
digraphs that can spell more than one sound:	*ch, th*

Set #22, page 79

Possible responses:

1.	**ch sounds like /k/:** chameleon, chemist, choir, cholesterol
	ch sounds /sh/: chalet, Charlotte, chauffeur, chef
	ch sounds like /ch/: cheese, cherry, chicken, chimpanzee
	Additional words:
	ch sounds like /k/: choreography, cholera, chasm, chameleon, charisma
	ch sounds /sh/: Cheyenne, chateau, chaparral, chanticleer, chaise lounge
	ch sounds like /ch/: chess, cheddar, Chinese, chapter, chinchilla
2.	**th sounds like /th/:** thank-you, thaw, thief, thistle, thunder
	th sounds like /th/: the, then, these, they, though
	Additional words:
	th sound like /th/: thick, thermometer, thrill, thesaurus, theater
	th sounds like /th/: thy, that, themselves, there, they'd

Set #23, page 80

Answers will vary. Possible responses:

bl	blond, blood, blimp, bloated, black
br	brown, brawny, bruised, brooding, Brahman
cl	clown, closet, cloister, cloudy, clunk
cr	crumpet, cruise, crooked, crocodile, Creole
dr	drip, drum, dreadful, dromedary, droll
fl	Florida, flippers, floral, flea, flowing
fr	Frisbee, fry, fraud, frazzled, frosting
gl	gloat, glad, glutton, gloaming, glacier
gr	green, grab, gruesome, grueling, gravel
pl	plunk, plank, plink, plumber, plywood
pr	predator, prune, prominent, pragmatic, prairie dog
sc	scattered, scapegoat, scuttle, scab, scone
scr	scram, scream, scrap, scrape, scrimshaw
sk	skunk, skim, skillet, skeleton, ski
sl	slam, slang, slippery, slap, sloop
sm	smash, smithereens, smuggle, smelly, smorgasbord
sn	sneeze, snort, snicker, sneer, snigger
sp	spell, spittoon, spawn, spangled, spider
spr	spring, sprightly, spruce, sprinkles, spray
st	stab, stirrup, stellar, staring, steal
str	stream, stripe, strobe, strum, strong
sw	swipe, sweet, swell, swagger, swing
tr	trivia, treehouse, trapper, triangular, tragedy
tw	twerp, tweet, twister, twirl, tweak
wh	(Note: Not everyone pronounces *wh* as a blend.) whale, wharf, what, where, why

Set #24, page 80

Possible response:

They are all blends composed of a digraph and *r*.

Set #25, page 81

Possible responses:

ch peach
ph telegraph
sc disc

sh shush
sk disk
sm chasm

sp grasp
st forest
th forsooth

Set #26, page 82

Possible responses:

ft	lt	nd	nt	tch
ld	mp	ng	rd	ts

Set #27, page 82

Possible responses:

two blends or digraphs that make the same sound:	sc/sk tch/ch tz/ts
digraph that makes two different sounds:	ch
t blends:	ft lt nt st ts tz
s blends:	sc sk sp st ts
digraphs:	ch ng ph sh tch th

Set #28, page 83

Possible responses:

ch words with Vr:	torch, perch, arch, birch, lurch
ch words with Vn:	conch, bench, pinch, ranch, scrunch
ch words with V:	rich, much, loch, attach
ch words with VV:	pouch, peach, pooch, poach, screech
ch words with VVC:	haunch, search
tch words with V:	watch, witch, etch, Dutch, Scotch

Set #29, page 83

Possible responses:

ft	theft, raft, drift, aloft, tuft
ld	scald, held, gild, bold, guild
lt	halt, pelt, gilt, bolt, guilt
mp	damp, hemp, limp, chomp, bump

nd	wand, wend, wind, bond, cummerbund
ng	tang, zing, gong, lung, sling
nk	yank, fink, plonk, skunk, oink
nt	rant, accent, flint, don't, blunt
ph	graph, aleph, hieroglyph, humph, triumph
rd	weird, beard, bird, cord, curd
sh	ash, mesh, wish, gosh, blush
sk	mask, desk, risk, kiosk, rusk
sp	clasp, wisp, cusp, hasp, grasp
st	fast, fest, fist, cyst, dust
th	bath, Elizabeth, pith, sooth, truth
ts	gnats, bets, kits, plots, guts
tz	ersatz, klutz

Set #30, page 84

Possible responses:

depth	blend of p and digraph th
search	blend of r and digraph ch
hearts	blend of r, t, and s
tenth	blend of n and digraph th
harsh	blend of r and digraph sh

CHAPTER FOUR

Vowel Sounds

We usually represent vowel sounds . . . but there is more to the story.

SHORT VOWEL SOUNDS

What is a vowel?

The vowels in English are *a, e, i, o, u,* and sometimes *y,* right? Not quite! Remember, a vowel is not a letter—it's a sound during which air flows from your throat through and out of your mouth without being stopped. If the air is partially or completely cut off during a sound, then you've made a consonant sound.

The letters named above USUALLY represent vowel sounds. But there are exceptions. Sometimes letters we have come to think of as "vowels" may represent consonant sounds. For example, the letter *u* often represents the consonant sound /w/, as in the word *quiet.* And sometimes the letters we think of as consonants help to represent vowel sounds, as in the word *delight,* where the letters *i, g,* and *h* work together to display a vowel sound /ī/, according to one explanation.

We classify English vowel sounds into groups to make it easier to think and talk about them. Common groupings include: **short vowels, long vowels, r-controlled vowels,** and **diphthongs.** We are going to talk about each of these groups in separate sections to help you focus.

A vowel is not a letter?

Introducing . . . (drumroll) the shorts

The letters *a*, *e*, *i*, *o*, and *u* each correspond to a "short" sound (short because it sounds for a shorter time, so it's said). The short vowel sounds are heard in the following words:

a c**a**t   **e** b**e**dbug   **i** **i**guana   **o** grassh**o**pper   **u** b**u**tterfly

But wait! Stop! Hold everything! Not everybody pronounces these sounds the same way. To understand more, try this experiment.

BRAIN TICKLERS
Set #31 Analyze Your Own Pronunciation

1. Say all of these words out loud to yourself. Make lists (as many as you need) to show the different vowel pronunciations you use when you say the bold-faced letters. Note: There is no right or wrong answer. Just divide the words into the categories YOU use.

all   **aw**ful   ba**h**   baz**aa**r   b**o**re   b**ough**t   c**a**ll   c**augh**t
c**aw**   ch**a**lk   c**o**d   c**o**llar   c**o**t   d**augh**ter   f**a**ther   fr**o**g
gn**aw**   g**ua**rd   guit**a**r   h**ea**rt   h**o**nor   h**o**rse   kn**ow**ledge
l**a**undry   l**o**t   p**o**t   qu**a**lity   sal**a**mi   s**au**ce   s**er**geant
st**a**lk   t**au**t   t**o**t   wharf

2. Now look at the pronunciation lists in *The American Heritage Dictionary*. Compare and contrast your groups with the dictionary's groups. What observations can you make? Now compare your answers with the *Merriam Webster's* groupings.

3. Now classify each of your groups according to the spellings of the vowel sound. Briefly explain your classifications.

(Answers are on page 106.)

More about dialect

People in different parts of the United States (and elsewhere) who speak English pronounce words somewhat differently, depending on the **dialect** that they speak. A dialect is a subset of a language, usually confined to a particular region. But African American English is an example of a dialect that is NOT regionalized. There are three main dialect areas in the United States: Northern, Southern, and Midland. But the differences in pronunciation are so specific that a language specialist could listen to you and tell whether you are from the Northern Middle West; New England; Chicago; the Central Atlantic Seaboard; Gary, Indiana; the Southern Coast; New York City; and so on. No particular dialect is better than any other dialect, although some may be more popular than others, or people may CLAIM that theirs is superior.

The differences in dialect are noticeable when you listen to the way words like *father* and *hot* are pronounced. In any dictionary you check, you will probably find some words shown with /ä/ that you pronounce /ŏ/ and vice versa. And dictionaries are by no means in agreement about the number one spelling for these words.

Compared to this, /ă/, /ĕ/, and /ĭ/ are EASY.

BRAIN TICKLERS
Set #32 Find and Group Spellings of Short A, E, and I

1. For the sounds /ă/, /ĕ/, and /ĭ/, find as many different spellings as you can and write a word that has each spelling. You may use the chart on page 49 for help, but for every spelling you include from the chart, add another word in English that has that spelling and isn't on the chart, if you can.

2a. Group the /ă / spellings you found into categories that make sense to you. Write a sentence or two explaining your categories.

b. Now do the same for /ĕ /.

c. Time to repeat the procedure for /ĭ /.

(Answers are on pages 107–108.)

Time out for an explanation

To prepare for talking about short *u*, we need to introduce a couple of terms. Don't worry! You've probably heard these before. The first one is **syllable**. A syllable is a vowel sound, either by itself or with the preceding and following consonant sounds. The word *syllable* has three distinct syllables: syl la ble. How many syllables in *antidisestablishmentarianism?* Twelve (check it out).

All stressed out

Do you know what a **stressed syllable** is? No, it's not one that's had a really hard day. When we say words, we usually say one part more loudly than any other part. That's the **primary stress**.

In the word *metropolis*, we say *trop* louder than the rest. That's the primary stress. In the word *discombobulate* (it means to upset something or mess something up), we say *bob* the loudest, but *dis* and *late*, although softer than *bob*, are louder than *com* and *u*. That's called **secondary stress**. Try saying it yourself.

One way to represent stress is with little stress flags. Primary stress has a thicker, darker flag than secondary stress. Dictionaries use this system.

o′ ver worked′

Uhhhhhhh

When the sound of short *u* appears in a word in a stressed syllable like *butterfly*, we call it "short *u*." But in a lot of English words, a sound like short *u* appears in unstressed syllables. When such a sound appears in an UN-stressed syllable, we call the sound a **schwa** and represent it with this symbol: ə.

The word *schwa* comes from a Syriac word meaning "equal"— maybe because many different sounds are kind of "equalized" into one sound (more or less) in unstressed syllables. Here are some examples that will show you how sounds are equalized:

> *tyrannical* (short *a* /ă/) → *tyrant* (schwa /ə/)
> *telegraphy* (short *e* /ĕ/) → *telegraph* (schwa /ə/)
> *methodical* (short *o* /ŏ/) → *method* (schwa /ə/)
> *combine* (long *i* /ī/) → *combination* (schwa /ə/)
> *medicinal* (short *i* /ĭ/) → *medicine* (schwa /ə/)

Get the idea?

If you try saying the words with the schwa sounds, you may notice that your pronunciation of that sound is not exactly the same in all the words. That's the way English works: Sounds are affected by their context: the letters before and after them, whether they appear in a stressed or unstressed syllable, and so on.

BRAIN TICKLERS
Set #33 Musical Instruments Word Search

Hidden in this word search are the names of nine musical instruments. Three of the instruments have only a short *u* sound /ŭ/. Four of them have only a schwa /ə/ sound. Two of them have both a short *u* /ŭ/ AND a schwa /ə/. Words are horizontal, vertical, or diagonal and may be forward or backward. Find the words and group them in the proper categories.

S	I	U	S	R	I	P	E	C	O	R	O	C	U	P	T	R	M

S I U S R I P E C O R O C U P T R M
S C R D P E T O C L C R D L E E E A
A L M I O R D X X T A O U O T N C D
N O I S S U C R E P U L L R U I O O
O M R U S O B P O N E T C I N R R U
H U U I D D M L I C P O I O M A D B
P R A L N U O D E H E X M D I L I C
O D C L R M B T O B X R E C C C O I
S S I T C U E C U S A B R E I R U N
S S N T O N C O R H U S E R S X O P
X A O D E N O H P O X A S U N E T M
A B N I R P H O D D U L C O R I O U

(Answers are on page 108.)

BRAIN TICKLERS
Set #34 Categorize Short Vowel Words

1. Sort these short vowel words into groups that make sense to you. Write a sentence or two explaining your categories.

   business   calf   dog   dread   necessary
   giraffe   gnat   guest   guild   marriage
   twit

2. Compare these word pairs in which some of the letters are identical. What do you find?

   business/buster
   calf/halt
   dog/ogre
   dread/mead
   necessary/far
   guest/glue
   guild/ennui (This means "boredom"; it's pronounced / ŏn wē´/.)

3. Sort these short a /ă/ words into groups that make sense to you. Write a sentence or two explaining your categories.

   babble   bad   baffle   bag   battle   can   cattle
   haggle   ham   hassle   man   paddle   rat   stammer
   zap

4. Now add short e /ĕ/, short i /ĭ/, short o /ŏ/, and short u /ŭ/ words to each category you made, if possible.

   (Answers are on pages 108–109).

LONG VOWEL SOUNDS

O, I long 4 u

In this section we are going to talk about the sounds called long
a /ā/, long /ē/, long *i* /ī/, long *o* /ō/, and long *u* /ū/. The long vowel
sounds are the sounds that you hear when you say the names of
the letters *a, e, i, o,* and *u* PLUS the sound /o͞o/ without the /y/
sound. Even though long *u* has a consonant sound /y/ at the beginning, for example, in the word *cute*, we still call it a vowel
sound. As you know, both from your own experience and from
the chart in Chapter 2 (page 16 and following), long vowel
sounds are not always spelled with the letter whose name you
hear. In fact, some of them have some pretty strange spellings.

Taste your vowels

We usually don't think too much about how vowels feel in our mouths. But if you try these experiments, you'll learn something.

BRAIN TICKLERS
Set #35 More About Long and Short Vowels

1. Say *beet, boot, bait, boat, bite*. Notice how your lips move in and out. Describe what happens.

2. Say *bait, boat,* and *bite*, one at a time, and try to hold the vowel sound for a long time. Describe what happens.

3. Say the names of the letters *e, a, i*. How does your mouth position change as you move through the three vowel sounds?

4. Say the short vowels /ă/, /ĕ/, /ĭ/, /ŏ/, /ŭ/. Describe how your mouth changes. Now say the long vowels /ā/, /ē/, /ī/, /ō/, /ū/. Describe how your mouth changes. How were the two sets different?

(Answers are on page 109.)

Now let's see if you can pick out the long vowels by sound (and feel).

BRAIN TICKLERS
Set #36 Categorize Short and Long Vowel Words

Sort this list into words with short vowel sounds and words with long vowel sounds.

bread   seat
flat   flavor
oven   to
he   met
lemonade   comrade
crumb   truth
gauge   laugh
people   leopard
human   but
bit   wild
soon   flood
gym   my
you   trouble

The short and long vowels are spelled the same way in each pair of words, so watch out!

(Answers are on page 109.)

BRAIN TICKLERS
Set #37 Analyze Vowel and Consonant Patterns

Use the symbols V for "vowel" letter and C for "consonant" letter (in combination if necessary) to show patterns of spelling for long vowels /ā/, /ē/, /ī/, /ō/, /yōō/, and /ōō/ that occur in the words in Set #36. Show the pattern for the entire syllable that the long vowel appears in. Then brainstorm to find other patterns of two to six vowel and consonant letters that can convey syllables with long vowel sounds. Next to each pattern you identify, write a word that has the same pattern.

(Answers are on page 110.)

BRAIN TICKLERS
Set #38 Find Different Spellings for Long Vowel Sounds

For the sounds of long *a, e, i, o,* and the two forms of long *u* (/yōō/ and /ōō/), find as many different spellings as you can and write a word that has that spelling. You may use the chart on pages 49–54 for help, but for every spelling you include from the chart, also include a different word in English that has that spelling, if you can find one.

(Answers are on pages 110–112.)

BRAIN TICKLERS
Set #39 Find Homophones
for Given Words

Homophones are words that sound the same but are spelled differently, like *meat* and *meet*. Here is a list of some words with a long vowel sound, each of which has at least one homophone. Write the homophone(s) for each.

1. ale
2. isle
3. bail
4. base
5. Bea
6. beech
7. bow
8. boulder
9. bold

10. breech
11. brake
12. brood
13. bridle
14. buy
15. sealing
16. cheep
17. choose
18. site

19. creek
20. cruise
21. daze
22. due
23. dye
24. dough
25. does (several female deer)

Read more about homophones in Chapter 9.

(Answers are on page 112.)

BRAIN TICKLERS
Set #40 Homophones to Match

Read the definitions separated by semicolons. Write a set of long vowel homophones that matches each set of definitions.

1. a person who colors cloth; disastrous

2. the overhang at the edge of a roof; periods between dusk and night

3. the organ of sight; first person singular pronoun; how a sailor says "yes"

4. when a person loses consciousness; a move designed to trick someone

5. destiny; a celebration

6. a small insect that often lives on dogs; to run away

7. lets go from prison; to be very cold; a decorative band around the wall of a room

8. a chicken made especially for cooking in deep fat; a brother in a religious order

9. the pace of a horse; an entrance through a wall

10. to create fine powder out of hard cheese; wonderful and outstanding

(Answers are on page 112.)

BRAIN TICKLERS
Set #41 Find Homophones with Long Vowels

How many sets of homophones can you find with different spellings of the same long vowel? (No fair using homophones used in Brain Ticklers Sets #39 and #40.)

Get 10 and you're good.
Get 20 and you're an expert.
Get 30 or more and you're out of this world!

(Answers are on page 113.)

BRAIN TICKLERS—THE ANSWERS

Set #31, page 94

1. Here are some possible responses based on two dictionaries:

	American Heritage	**Merriam-Webster's**
Group 1	all awful bore bought call caught caw chalk daughter frog gnaw horse laundry sauce stalk taut wharf	all awful bought call caught caw chalk daughter frog gnaw horse laundry sauce stalk taut wharf
Group 2	bah bazaar father guard guitar heart salami sergeant	bore
Group 3	cod collar cot honor knowledge lot pot quality tot	bah bazaar cod collar cot father guard guitar heart honor knowledge lot pot quality salami sergeant tot

2. Answers will vary. You might conclude that pronunciation of these closely related sounds is highly irregular and hard to categorize.

3. Possible response (based on *American Heritage* groupings):
   Most short *o* words are spelled with an *o*, and most are CVC words.
   /ô/ can be spelled *a, aw, o_e, ough, augh, aw, al, o, au*.
   /ä/ can be spelled *ah, aa, a, a(r), ea(r), e(r)*.

Set #32, page 96

1. Possible responses:

short a *a* rat *au* aunt	*a_ _e* dance *i* timbre	*al* calf
short e *a* many *ea* sweat *u* burial	*ai* again *ei* heifer *ue* guest	*e* debt *eo* jeopardy
short i *a_e* courage *ia* marriage *y* crystal	*e* pretty *u* business	*i* snit *ui* built

2. Possible responses:

a. /ă/

One letter spellings: a, i a_e, ai, au	Multiple letter spellings:
a as in *rat*	**a_ _e** as in *dance*
i as in *timbre*	**al** as in *calf*
	au as in *aunt*

b. /ĕ/

Spellings with e in them: e, ea, ei, eo	Spellings without e in them: a, ai, u
e as in *debt*	**a** as in *many*
ea as in *sweat*	**ai** as in *again*
ei as in *heifer*	**u** as in *burial*
eo as in *jeopardy*	

c. /ĭ/

Spellings with i in them: i, ia, ui	Spellings without i in them: a_e, e, u, y
i as in *snit*	**a_e** as in *courage*
ia as in *marriage*	**e** as in *pretty*
ui as in *built*	**u** as in *business*
	y as in *crystal*

Set #33, page 98

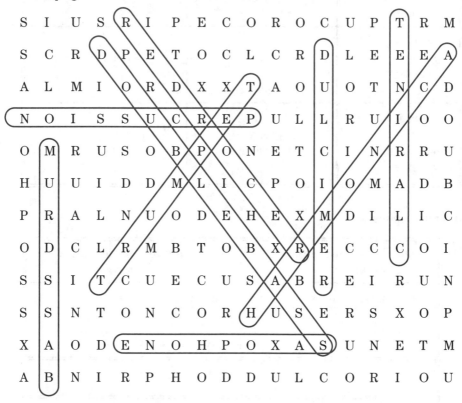

short *u* /ŭ/: tr**u**mpet, d**ou**ble bass, bass dr**u**m
schwa /ə/: harmonic**a**, sax**o**phone, clarin**e**t, record**er**
both: perc**u**ssi**o**n, d**u**lcimer

Set #34, page 99

1. Possible responses:
    short i words: business (spelled *u* and *e*), guild (spelled *ui*), marriage (spelled *ia*), twit (spelled *i*), giraffe (spelled *i*)

short a words: calf (spelled *al*), gnat (spelled *a*), giraffe (spelled *a_e*)
short e words: necessary (spelled *e* and *a*), dread (spelled *ea*), guest
(spelled *ue*)

2. In each case the identical letters represent different sounds in the two
   different words.

3. Possible responses:
   CVC words with short vowels: bad, bag, can, ham, man, rat, zap
   words with short vowels followed by a double consonant: babble,
   baffle, battle, cattle, haggle, hassle, paddle, stammer

4. Possible responses:
   CVC words with short vowels: fed, lid, cod, mud
   words with short vowels followed by a double consonant: tessellate,
   hiss, bottle, snuggle

Set #35, page 101

Your descriptions may be a little different than these, but you'll get the
general idea:

1. Lips are pulled back as in a grin for *bee*, *bait*, and *bite*; rounded and
   forward for *boot* and *boat*.

2. You cannot hold the vowel sound because it's actually made up of two different sounds. The technical term for this (in case you don't remember) is
   diphthong. It may also be called a *vowel glide*.

3. It opens progressively wider for each vowel.

4. Answers will vary. For the short vowels, the sound seems to come from
   about the same place in the back of my mouth, but my lips and jaw move
   around to change the vowel. For the long vowels, the sound seems to
   come from farther forward in my mouth, and just as for the short vowels,
   my lips and jaw move around to change the vowel. The short vowels and
   long vowels seem to be in different places in my mouth.

Set #36, page 102

Short: bread, flat, oven, met, comrade, crumb, laugh, leopard, but, bit,
flood, gym, trouble
Long: seat, flavor, to, he, lemonade, truth, gauge, people, human, wild, soon,
my, you

Set #37, page 103

Here are the words from Set #35:

seat CVVC	**truth** CCVCC	**human** CV
flavor CCV	**gauge** CVVCV	**wild** CVCC
my, to, he CV	**you, people** CVV	**soon** CVVC
lemonade VCV		

Here are words and patterns arranged in increasing length (answers will vary):

CV my	**CVCC** comb	**CVVCC** heist
VC I'm	**CVVC** coat	**CVVCe** cause
CVV jay	**CVVV** beau	**CVVVC** Seoul
CCV cry	**CVCe** cone	**CCVCC** brush
VVV eau (it comes from the French word for "water")	**CVCCe** waste	**CCVCCC** bright

Set #38, page 103

Possible responses:
Reminder: I have used the term *Oddball* to refer to a rare spelling, maybe even a unique spelling in English. I have not been able to find a definitive list of all possible English spellings for each sound.

Long a /ā/

a as in *flavor* **a_e** as in *tame* **a_ _e** as in *taste* **ae** as in *sundae* **ai** as in *rain* **ai_e** as in *plaice* (It's a fish, and Rudyard Kipling mentions it in the story "How the Whale Got His Throat.")	**aigh** ODDBALL Can you think of anything besides *straight?* **au** ODDBALL Can you think of anything besides *gauge?* **ay** as in br*ay* **é** as in *café* **e_e** as in *fete* **ea** as in *steak*	**ee** as in *toupee* **ei** as in *sheik* **eigh** as in *sleigh* **et** as in *croquet* **ey** as in *obey*

Long e /ē/

ae as in *aegis*	**eo** ODDBALL	**is** as in *ambergris*
ay as in *hurray*	Can you think of	(second pronun-
e as in *aborigine*	anything besides	ciation from
e_e as in *athlete*	*people?*	*Merriam Web-*
ea as in *pea*	**ey** as in *monkey*	*ster's Collegiate*
ea_e as in *grease*	**i** as in *kiwi*	*Dictionary*)
ee as in *employee*	**i_e** as in	**oe** as in *Phoebe*
ei as in *protein*	*automobile*	**y** as in *uncanny*
	ie as in *achieve*	

Long i /ī/

ai as in *naiad* and	**ay** as in *cayenne*	**is** as in *isle*
Shanghai—and	(very rare	**oy** ODDBALL
that's it, accord-	spelling)	Can you think of
ing to Edward	**ei** as in	anything besides
Carney in *A*	*kaleidoscope*	*coyote?*
Survey of	**eigh** as in *sleight*	**ui_e** ODDBALL
English	**ey** as in *geyser*	Can you think of
Spelling	(very rare	anything besides
ais Carney says	spelling)	*guide?*
aisle is the	**i** as in *alibi*	**y** as in *wry*
only English	**i_e** as in *crime*	**ye** as in *rye*
word with this	**ie** as in *pie*	**y_e** as in *thyme*
spelling.	**igh** as in *knight*	

Long o /ō/

au as in *chauffeur*	**oa** as in *hoax*	Note: Here are
eau as in *bureau*	**oe** as in *toe*	some other
eo ODDBALL	**oh** as in *Shiloh*	oddball /o/
Can you think of	**ol** as in *molt*	spellings, just
anything besides	**ou** as in *boulder*	for you:
yeoman?	**ough** as in *dough*	**aoh**—as in
ew ODDBALL	**ow** as in *bungalow*	*pharaoh*
Can you think of	**owe** ODDBALL	**eou**—as in *Seoul*
anything besides	Can you think of	**oo**—as in
sew?	anything besides	*Roosevelt*
o as in *burro*	*owe(s)?*	
o_e as in *nose*		

VOWEL SOUNDS

Long u /o͞o/

eu as in *rheumatism* **ew** as in *grew* **ho** as in *whom* **o** as in *tomb* **oo** as in *raccoon* **o_e** as in *lose*	**oe** as in *shoe* (very rare) **ou** as in *croup* **ough** ODDBALL Can you think of anything besides *through?* **u** as in *gnu*	**u_e** as in *prune* **ue** as in *glue* **ui** as in *bruise* **wo** ODDBALL Can you think of anything besides *two?*

Long u /yo͞o/

eau ODDBALL Can you think of anything besides *beauty?*	**ew** as in *nephew* **iew** as in *view* **u** as in *unity*	**ue** as in *argue* **u_e** as in *huge*

Set #39, page 104

1. ail
2. aisle
3. bale
4. bass
5. be, bee
6. beach
7. beau/bough
8. bolder
9. bowled
10. breach
11. break
12. brewed
13. bridal
14. by
15. ceiling
16. cheap
17. chews
18. cite, sight
19. creak
20. crews
21. days
22. dew
23. die
24. doe
25. doze

Set #40, page 105

1. dyer, dire
2. eaves, eves
3. eye, I, aye
4. faint, feint
5. fate, fete
6. flea, flee
7. frees, freeze, frieze
8. fryer, friar
9. gait, gate
10. grate, great

Set #41, page 106

Possible responses:
1. gale, Gail
2. greys, graze
3. groan, grown
4. grosser, grocer
5. guys, guise
6. heal, heel
7. hew, hue
8. higher, hire
9. hoes, hose
10. knave, nave
11. knead, need
12. knew, new
13. know, no
14. knows, nose
15. liar, lyre
16. load, lode
17. loan, lone
18. made, maid
19. male, mail
20. mane, main
21. maze, maize
22. moat, mote
23. mooed, mood
24. mowed, mode
25. night, knight
26. owed, ode
27. paced, paste
28. pail, pale
29. pain, pane
30. peace, piece
31. peak, peek, pique
32. peal, peel
33. pi, pie

34. plaice, place
35. plane, plain
36. pleas, please
37. pray, prey
38. pried, pride
39. pries, prise, prize
40. pros, prose
41. read, reed
42. road, rode
43. roe, row
44. roes, rows, rose
45. role, roll
46. roomer, rumor
47. rues, ruse
48. sail, sale
49. scene, seen
50. sea, see
51. seam, seem
52. sew, so, sow
53. shone, shown
54. shoot, chute
55. sighed, side
56. sighs, size
57. sign, sine
58. slay, sleigh
59. sleight, slight
60. sold, soled
61. sole, soul, Seoul
62. stake, steak
63. stayed, staid
64. steal, steel
65. stile, style
66. straight, strait
67. suite, sweet

68. swayed, suede
69. tail, tale
70. tea, tee
71. team, teem
72. teas, tease
73. throne, thrown
74. through, threw
75. tied, tide
76. toe, tow
77. towed, toad
78. vain, vane, vein
79. vale, veil
80. wait, weight
81. waste, waist
82. wave, waive
83. way, weigh
84. we've, weave
85. we, wee
86. weak, week
87. weighed, wade
88. whale, wail
89. wheel, weal
90. while, wile
91. whiled, wild
92. whined, wind
93. whole, hole
94. who's, whose
95. wreak, reek
96. wright, write, right, rite
97. wrote, rote
98. yoke, yolk
99. you, ewe, yew

CHAPTER FIVE

More Challenging Spelling Patterns

MISCELLANEOUS VOWEL SOUNDS

R—The control freak

Have you ever heard the term *control freak* for someone who has to dominate the situation? Well, when the letter *r* comes after a vowel, it usually exerts some power over it, changing its sound, so that we call such vowels *r-controlled*, or *r-influenced*, or *rhotic* vowels.

BRAIN TICKLERS
Set #42 Analyze R-Controlled Vowels

In each pair of words the first letter and the vowels are the same. But in one word, the letter *r* follows the vowel(s), and in the other, there is no *r*. Compare each set of words: do they have the same vowel sounds, or different vowel sounds?

fork, fold
fur, fun
girl, give
herd, help
mirage, mileage

park, pack
tore, tone
wear, wean
work, won't

(Answers are on page 128.)

BRAIN TICKLERS
Set #43 Categorize Words with R-Controlled Vowels

1. Sort the words below into groups that have the same vowel sound.

sphere   warm   four   wear
were   worm   fir   steer
fear   wore   fair   fur
dare

2. Add three words of your own choosing to each group you formed.

(Answers are on page 128.)

R u ready for this?

Vowel sounds influenced by the letter *r* following them are shown as wearing little hats called circumflexes (ˆ). There are four of them: /âr/, /îr/, /ôr/, and /ûr/.

Char has the sound /âr/.
Cheer has the sound /îr/.
Chore has the sound /ôr/.
Chirp has the sound /ûr/.

Other vowel sounds can appear before the letter *r* as well. You can have /ōr/, /īr/, /o͞or/ (see what follows for more about this sound), and so on. If you don't see a hat on the letter in the pronunciation, then pronounce it in the way indicated: long, short, or what have you.

BRAIN TICKLERS
Set #44 Final Varied Spellings for R-Controlled Vowels

For the sounds of /âr/, /îr/, /ôr/, and /ûr/ find as many different spellings as you can and write a word that has each spelling. You may use the chart on page 51 for help, but for every spelling you include from the chart, add a word in English (if you can find one) that uses that same spelling but isn't on the chart. Skip over the oddballs.

SOUND	SPELLING		
	COMMON	**UNUSUAL**	**ODDBALL**
/âr/			**ayer** as in *prayer* **eir** as in *heir*
/îr/			**aer** as in *aerie*–2nd **eor** as in *theory* **eyr** as in *eyrie*–2nd **iere** as in *premiere* **ière** as in *première* **yr** as in *Tyr*
/ôr/			**awr** as in *Lawrence* **oer** as in *Boer*–2nd **orr** as in *torr*
/ûr/			**ere** as in *were* **irr** as in *whirr* **olo** as in *colonel* **or** as in *work* **our** as in *courtesy* **yrrh** as in *myrrh*

(Answers are on pages 128–129.)

What's left?

Are we done with the vowels yet? Well, not quite. A couple of diphthongs aren't included in the long vowel category, and one other sound seems to hang out all by itself. First, the diphthongs:

/oi/ is the vowel sound in the word *boy*.
/ou/ is the vowel sound in the word *ow*.

Easy, huh?

The other sound is represented by the symbol /o͞o/, and you hear it in the word *put*.

Now try this sorting exercise.

BRAIN TICKLERS
Set #45 Categorize Words with OU and OI

1. Sort these words into groups according to the sound of the bold letters.

av**oi**d	g**oo**d	s**oy**
d**ou**bt	H**ow**ard	t**oo**k
empl**oy**	p**ou**t	w**ou**ld

2. Add three words of your own choosing to each group.

(Answers are on page 129.)

"SILENT" LETTERS

Shhhhhh! Silent letter zone

Some people talk about letters that are not heard making their "usual" sound in a word as *silent*. Other people prefer to talk about these letters in other ways. Edward Carney, author of *A Survey of English Spelling*, distinguishes two kinds of *silent* letters: *auxiliary* and *dummy*.

Auxiliary letters are actually digraphs; they are combinations of letters that spell sounds that do not have a usual single letter to represent them. For example:
/*th*/ thing
/th/ there
/sh/ share
/zh/ treasure
/ng/ song

Dummy letters do not have the same kind of function that auxiliary letters do. There are two different subgroups of dummy letters. **Inert letters** are letters that appear as part of a letter sequence with a particular meaning even when they're not pronounced (inert). For more on this type of letter group (called *morphemes*), see page 157. For example, the *g* in *resignation* is heard. In resign it's inert. Similarly the *g* in *malignant* is heard. In *malign*, it's inert.

That dummy hasn't made a sound.

You can see that the *g* is visually important in recognizing the connection between the words (that is, the word segment is the same in both cases so we know the meanings are related), even though it is pronounced in one instance and not in the other. We'll learn more about this in Chapter 8.

Empty letters are letters that seem to do absolutely nothing. They do not have a function like auxiliary letters or inert letters. The letter *u* in the word *gauge* is empty. If the word was spelled *gage*, we could read and spell it perfectly well.

Finally, final e

Since we are in a vowel chapter (at least so far), let's start with the most notorious silent letter of them all—silent *e* at the end of a word with a long vowel sound. What's it doing there, anyway? Well, it's there as a marker to tell you that the vowel is long, that's what. **Markers** are letters that do not represent a sound themselves, but that tell us something about the sound of other letters in the word. Final silent *e* is an example of a marker. It signals a long vowel sound in the syllable it finishes. You can tell the difference between

- *mat* and *mate*
- *hat* and *hate*
- *rot* and *rote*
- *fat* and *fate*
- *not* and *note*
- *cut* and *cute*

and so on, because the *e* is marking long vowels for you.

BRAIN TICKLERS
Set #46 Find Pairs of Short and Long Vowel Words

Make ten sets like those above: two one-syllable words, one of which has a short vowel sound and the other of which has a final *e* to mark the vowel sound as long.

(Answers are on page 129.)

A final *e* can also tell you how to pronounce *th* in words like

breath and *breathe*
cloth and *clothe*
loath and *loathe*.

And, conversely, the pronunciation—/th/ or /*th*/—can tell you whether to spell the word with or without a final *e*.

BRAIN TICKLERS
Set #47 Find Words in Which Final E Shifts Pronunciation of the Digraph TH

Find three more pairs of words in which a final *e* helps you know how to pronounce the digraph *th*.

(Answers are on page 129.)

Double consonants

Well, you may point out, not all long vowels have an *e* to let you know how to pronounce them. You're right. Another way we recognize long vowels is that they're **not** followed by a double consonant, a sign that often lets us know that the sound of the preceding vowel is short. There are exceptions: *troll* with an /ō/ is one. But many if not most times, a double consonant at the end of a syllable means the syllable has a short vowel sound. (There are other reasons for doubling consonants that will be discussed later when we talk about endings.)

BRAIN TICKLERS
Set #48 List CVCC Words

Make a list of twenty CVCC words in which the double consonant marks the syllable as having a short vowel sound. One rule: the first letter of the two consonants that end the word CANNOT be an *r*. For example, don't use the words *hurt* or *barn*, which have *r* as the third letter.

(Answers are on page 130.)

Silent partners

On page 122 and elsewhere, we've looked at some consonants that are "silent" when they help to spell vowel sounds (at least, that's one way to interpret it). Remember these?

- **eigh** spells /ā/ in *neigh*bor
- **is** spells /ī/ in *island*
- **ow** spells /ō/ in *mow*
- **hou** spells /ou/ in *hour*

She's always helpful but never utters a sound.

That's one category of silent consonants. But another category is consonants that are silent but unconnected to a vowel sound (usually in a group of two consonants). Here are some examples:

- silent **b** in *comb*
- silent **h** in *ghost*
- silent **k** in *knight*
- silent **t** in *listen*
- silent **c** in *scissors*
- silent **w** in *wrong*

BRAIN TICKLERS
Set #49 Find Silent Consonants and Their Patterns

1. How many words can you list that have a silent consonant letter? I have a list of 168 in the answer section (by no means a complete list). Can you find . . . 30? (NO DOUBLE LETTERS, e.g., mm, bb, and so on, ALLOWED IN THIS GAME!!) Hint: letters to focus on: *b, d, g, h, k, p, t, w*

2. Write briefly about any patterns you find.

(Answers are on pages 130–132.)

BRAIN TICKLERS—THE ANSWERS

Set #42, page 118

None of the sets of the words share the same vowel sound.

Set #43, page 118

1. Possible response (it may vary depending on your dialect):
   - sphere, steer, fear
   - warm, wore, four
   - worm, fir, fur, were
   - daire, dare, wear

2. Additional word possibilities:
   - mere, near, gear
   - door, floor, more, core
   - brrr, stir, her, incur
   - hair, bear, Claire, mare

Set #44, page 120

Possible responses:

SOUND	SPELLING		
	COMMON	UNUSUAL	ODDBALL
/âr/	**air** as in *fair* **ar** as in *librarian* **are** as in *hare* **ear** as in *bear*	**aer** as in *aerosol* **aire** as in *solitaire* **er** as in *sombrero*	**ayer** as in *prayer* **eir** as in *heir*
/îr/	**ear** as in *sear* **eer** as in *sneer* **er** as in *hero* **ere** as in *revere*	**eir** as in *weir* **ier** as in *pier*	**aer** as in *aerie*–2nd **eor** as in *theory* **eyr** as in *eyrie*–2nd **iere** as in *premiere* **ière** as in *première* **yr** as in *Tyr*

/ôr/	**ar** as in *warn*	**aur** as in *dinosaur*	**awr** as in *Lawrence*
	or as in *forest*	**oar** as in *boar*	**oer** as in *Boer*–2nd
	ore as in *ignore*	**oor** as in *floor*	**orr** as in *torr*
		our as in *pour*	
/ûr/	**er** as in *refer*	**ear** as in *earn*	**ere** as in *were*
	eur as in *entrepreneur*	**urr** as in *purr*	**irr** as in *whirr*
	ir as in *stir*	**yr** as in *myrtle*	**olo** as in *colonel*
	ur as in *burp*		**or** as in *work*
			our as in *courtesy*
			yrrh as in *myrrh*

Set #45, page 121

1. avoid, employ, soy
   - doubt, Howard, pout
   - good, took, would

2. Additional word possibilities:
   - coil, annoy, spoil
   - cloud, down, proud
   - book, could, foot

Set #46, page 124

Possible responses:

Nat and Nate	kin and kine
hug and huge	rat and rate
hid and hide	pop and pope
rag and rage	pan and pane
pin and pine	glad and glade

Set #47, page 125

Possible responses:
1. lath and lathe
2. wreath and wreathe
3. teeth and teethe
4. bath and bathe

Set #48, page 126

Possible responses include:

back	rent	mend	dump
pack	sent	fist	rump
tack	tent	gist	bath
camp	bend	list	math
damp	lend	bump	path
lamp			

Set #49, page 127

Answers will vary, depending on your dialect.

silent *b*			
bomb	debt	limb	thumb
catacomb	doubt	numb	tomb
climb	dumb	plumber	womb
comb	indebted	subtle	
crumb	lamb	succumb	

silent *c*			
Connecticut	muscle	scepter	Tucson
czar	scene	science	victual
indict	scent	scissors	

silent *ch*			
yacht			

silent *d*			
grandfather	grandpa	handsome	veldt
grandma	grandson	landscape	Wednesday
grandmother	handkerchief	sandwich	Windsor

silent *g*			
align	cologne	gnarled	malign
arraign	consign	gnash	paradigm
assign	deign	gnat	phlegm
benign	design	gnaw	poignant
bologna	diaphragm	gnome	reign
campaign	ensign	gnostic	resign
champagne	feign	gnu	sign
cognac	foreign	impugn	sovereign

silent *h*

aghast	ghetto	khaki	rhubarb
annihilate	ghost	myrrh	rhyme
cheetah	ghoul	pooh	rhythm
dinghy	hallelujah	rhapsody	sorghum
exhaust	heir	rhetoric	spaghetti
exhibit	herb	rheumatism	vehement
exhort	honest	rhinoceros	
ghastly	honor	rhizome	
gherkin	hour	rhododendron	

silent *k*

knack	knell	knit	knot
knave	knickers	knob	know
knead	knife	knock	knowledge
knee	knight	knoll	knuckle

silent *l*

calf	could	palm	talk
caulk	folk	salmon	walk
chalk	half	should	would

silent *m*

mnemonic

silent *n*

autumn	condemn	hymn
column	government	solemn

silent *p*

clapboard	pneumonia	psychiatry	raspberry
corps	psalm	psychology	receipt
coup	psalter	ptarmigan	
cupboard	pseudonym	pterodactyl	
pneumatic	psoriasis	ptomaine	

silent *t*

apostle	epistle	listen	ricochet
ballet	fasten	moisten	rustle
bristle	glisten	mortgage	soften
bustle	gourmet	nestle	thistle
castle	gristle	often	trestle
chasten	hasten	pestle	wrestle
christen	hustle	potpourri	
Christmas	jostle	rapport	

silent *w*

answer	wrangle	wrestle	write
sword	wrap	wretch	writhe
two	wrath	wriggle	wrong
who	wreak	wright	wrote
whole	wreath	wring	wrought
whose	wreck	wrinkle	wrung
wraith	wren	wrist	wry

Part Three

SYLLABLE JUNCTURES

CHAPTER SIX

Compound Words and Shortened Words

COMPOUND WORDS

Compound words are words made up of two or more whole words, not just word parts or elements. In this way, compound words are different from words with one or more affixes attached. *Antidisestablishmentarianism* is a long, sophisticated word, but it's not a compound word. It's a word with two prefixes, a base word, and four suffixes:

Prefixes **Base** **Suffixes**
Anti- dis- *establish* *-ment -arian (-ary + -an) -ism*

BRAIN TICKLERS
Set #50 Categorize Compound Words

Group the following compound words in categories that make sense to you. Write a sentence or two explaining your categories.

best seller
bridegroom
bull's-eye
cross-country skiing
emerald green
great-great-uncle
how-to book
ice cream

one-half mile
problem solving
stick-in-the-mud
toothache
vice-president
whiteout
whole-wheat bread

(Answers are on page 148.)

Biography of a compound

We generally distinguish three categories of compound words:

open (in which there is space between the words): ice cream

hyphenated (in which they are connected by a hyphen): merry-go-round

and

closed (in which the words are run together): playground

In general, compounds begin their life together just sitting next to each other in sentences. This casual association happens so often that people recognize it and make the relationship of the words more formal by putting a hyphen between them. As the relationship continues, the words are thought of in such close connection that they become joined forever.

It is my personal opinion that some compound words stay in the hyphen stage and never become closed simply because they would be too difficult to read closed up.

Like *merry-go-round, jack-in-the-pulpit* (a woodland plant) is a lot easier to read at a glance than *Jackinthepulpit*. Even its shorter name, *Indian turnip*, looks pretty funny stuck together: *Indianturnip*.

To hyphenate or not to hyphenate: that is the question

There are two different reasons why a particular set of words may be spelled with a hyphen at some times and not at others. First, some words that exist as compounds with a particular meaning can also appear together but not as a compound and with a very different meaning. In these cases, how you connect the words can give your sentence two VERY different interpretations. My favorite example is from *Words Into Type*, 3rd ed., page 227. Compare these two sentences:

She used a camel's-hair brush.
She used a camel's hairbrush.

Which would you rather use on your hair?

139

Sometimes capital letters can help distinguish a compound word.

He lives in the white house.

is way different from

He lives in the White House.

BRAIN TICKLERS
Set #51 Illustrate Compound Words

Draw a picture for each sentence.

1. Wow! What a hot house!
2. Wow! What a hothouse!
3. That man is my great-grandfather.
4. That man is my great grandfather.
5. The house full of people began to dance.
6. The houseful of people began to dance.
7. She is an ancient Chinese scholar.
8. She is an Ancient Chinese scholar.

(Answers are on page 149.)

The second reason that words may be spelled open in some cases and hyphenated in others is to help distinguish when they are used as different parts of speech. For example, a number of compounds are open when they're used as nouns and hyphenated when they're used as adjectives. This is done to help readers know which words go together.

Noun: Juan enjoys **mountain climbing**.

Adjective: Juan is going on a **mountain-climbing** expedition this summer.

Noun: Zach is making **chopped liver**.

Adjective: **Chopped-liver** appetizers sound grander if
they're called paté.

While it's important for you to know about the fact that
spelling can be different depending on the grammatical use of a
word, the rules for compounds is complicated. Your best
approach is to use a dictionary and/or spell-checker to make
sure you spell compound words accurately.

You can count on it

Although some compounds are spelled differently depending on
their grammatical use, and although many compound words go
through a progression, becoming more closely linked the longer
they stay together, some rules for compounds are always true.
And some of these more permanent rules are about using
hyphens with numbers. Here are four:

1. Spell all compound numbers from 21 to 99 with hyphens.

   twenty-one   *ninety-nine*

2. Spell all fractions used as adjectives with hyphens.

   two-thirds of a foot   *three-tenths* of a mile

3. Spell all compound adjectives that contain a cardinal number
   followed by a noun or adjective with hyphens.

   nine-foot board   *one-sided* argument

   two-hundred-dollar keyboard

4. Spell all compound adjectives that contain an ordinal number
   followed by a noun with a hyphen.

   third-story room   *first-class* accommodations

ABBREVIATIONS

English makes use of several shortened forms of words, chiefly abbreviations and contractions.

Abbreviations take two main forms. Some abbreviations begin with the first letter of the word, include a few other significant letters for a total of three or four, and often end with a period. These can be the first part of the word only, as in *adj.* for *adjective*, or include the final letter as well, as in *govt.* for *government*. Sometimes consonants from throughout the word are used, as in *blvd.* for *boulevard*. The idea is to shorten the form, while giving enough information that you can recognize the word without mistake.

Initialisms are abbreviations of phrases or compound words featuring the first letters of each of the words, or of all the important words. Some initialisms are written in all capital letters (*IRS* – Internal Revenue Service), and others are written all lower case (*scuba* – self-contained underwater breathing apparatus). Most initialisms, like IRS, are pronounced as a letter sequence. Initialisms that are pronounced as if they were a word, like *scuba*, are called **acronymns**.

COMMON ABBREVIATIONS

TIME			
A.M.	ante meridiem (12 midnight to 12 noon)	B.C.E.	Before the Common Era or Christian Era
P.M.	post meridiem (12 noon to 12 midnight)	C.E.	Common Era or Christian Era
		sec.	second
A.D.	Anno Domini (in the year of the Lord)	min.	minute
		h	hour
B.C.	Before Christ	hrs.	hours

DAYS AND DATES			
Days of the Week			
Sunday	Sun.	Thursday	Thurs.
Monday	Mon.	Friday	Fri.
Tuesday	Tues.	Saturday	Sat.
Wednesday	Wed.		
Months of the Year			
January	Jan.	July*	July
February	Feb.	August	Aug.
March	Mar.	September	Sept.
April	Apr.	October	Oct.
May*	May	November	Nov.
June*	June	December	Dec.

*no abbreviation

E-MAIL AND INSTANT MESSAGE			
afaik	as far as i know	imo	in my opinion
asap	as soon as possible	lol	laughing out loud
btw	by the way	np	no problem
fyi	for your information	tbd	to be determined
imho	in my humble opinion	tia	thanks in advance

STATE POSTAL ABBREVIATIONS

Alabama	AL	Louisiana	LA
Alaska	AK	Maine	ME
American Samoa	AS	Maryland	MD
Arizona	AZ	Massachusetts	MA
Arkansas	AR	Michigan	MI
California	CA	Minnesota	MN
Canal Zone	CZ	Mississippi	MS
Colorado	CO	Missouri	MO
Connecticut	CT	Montana	MT
Delaware	DE	Nebraska	NE
District of Columbia	DC	Nevada	NV
Florida	FL	New Hampshire	NH
Georgia	GA	New Jersey	NJ
Guam	GU	New Mexico	NM
Hawaii	HI	New York	NY
Idaho	ID	North Carolina	NC
Illinois	IL	North Dakota	ND
Indiana	IN	Ohio	OH
Iowa	IA	Oklahoma	OK
Kansas	KS	Oregon	OR
Kentucky	KY	Pennsylvania	PA

Puerto Rico	PR	Vermont	VT
Rhode Island	RI	Virgin Islands	VI
South Carolina	SC	Virginia	VA
South Dakota	SD	Washington	WA
Tennessee	TN	West Virginia	WV
Texas	TX	Wisconsin	WI
Utah	UT	Wyoming	WY

WRITING ABBREVIATIONS		
i.e. id est – that is	et al. et alia – and others	
e.g. exempli gratia – for example	etc. et cetera – and so on	

Notice that some abbreviations use periods and some don't. When in doubt, consult a dictionary.

CONTRACTIONS

Contractions, the other main kind of shortened word, are two words combined, but with several letters omitted (usually one or two). The missing letters are always indicated by the presence of an apostrophe '.

Most contractions are formed from combining a pronoun and a verb, a verb and a negative word, a question word and a verb, or a demonstrative pronoun and a form of the verb *to be*.

Following are charts of the most common contractions divided into these four categories.

COMMON CONTRACTIONS

Pronoun + Verb			
I'm	I am	she'd	she had, she would
I'll	I will	it's	it is
I've	I have	it'll	it will
I'd	I had, I would	it'd	it had, it would
you're	you are	we're	we are
you'll	you will	we'll	we will
you've	you have	we've	we have
you'd	you had, you would	we'd	we had, we would
he's	he is, he has	they're	they are
he'll	he will	they'll	they will
he'd	he had, he would	they've	they have
she's	she is, she has	they'd	they had, they would
she'll	she will		

Demonstrative Pronoun + Verb To Be			
here's	here is	there'll	there will, there shall
that's	that is	there've	there have
there's	there is		

Verb + Negative			
doesn't	does not	wouldn't	would not
don't	do not	can't	cannot
didn't	did not	couldn't	could not
hasn't	has not	mayn't	may not
haven't	have not	mustn't	must not
hadn't	had not	needn't	need not
isn't	is not	oughtn't	ought not
aren't	are not	shan't	shall not
wasn't	was not	shouldn't	should not
weren't	were not	daren't	dare not
won't	will not		

Question Word + Verb			
who's	who is	when's	when is
who'd	who would, who had	where's	where is
what's	what is	why'd	why did, why would

Don't confuse contractions with possessives, which also use apostrophes. Possessives don't have any letters left out; they simply indicate ownership.

BRAIN TICKLERS
Set #52 Form Compounds and Abbreviations from List

1. Form as many compounds as possible by combining words from the following list:

break	full	shine
day	light	stop
fast	moon	sun

2. Form as many contractions as possible by combining words from the following list:

am	are	will	have
I	you	would	not

(Answers are on page 150.)

BRAIN TICKLERS—THE ANSWERS

Set #50, page 137

Possible responses:
- best seller   emerald green   ice cream   problem solving
- bridegroom   toothache   whiteout
- bull's-eye   great-great-uncle   stick-in-the-mud   vice-president
- cross-country skiing   how-to book   one-half mile whole-wheat bread

Possible response:
Some of the compounds are run together, some have a space between them, some are connected by a hyphen, and some have a hyphen between two of their words and space between the other two.

Set #51, page 140

Answers in art:

1.

2.

3.

4.

5.

6.

7.

8.

Set #52, page 148

1. full moon   moonshine   sunshine
    full stop   stoplight   sunlight
    daylight   daybrea   breakfast
    fast day

2. I'm   I'll   I've   I'd
    you're you'll you've you'd
    aren't haven't won't   wouldn't

CHAPTER SEVEN

Affixes: Prefixes and Suffixes

SYLLABLE JUNCTURES WITH PREFIXES AND SUFFIXES

Now we're going to shift our focus from vowel and consonant sounds to a more visual approach for a while. We're going to look closely at the points in words where syllables meet, known as *syllable junctures*.

I'm heading down to Syllable Junctures.

We call it Sjs for short!

Variety is the spice of syllables

The basic way we characterize syllables is by the pattern of consonant letters and vowel letters that they contain.

BRAIN TICKLERS
Set #53 Match One-Syllable Word Patterns

Write five words for each one-syllable word pattern.

CV	CVCe	CVVC
CVC	CVCC	CCVV
CCV	CCVC	CVCCe
CVV		

(Answers are on page 186.)

What good is a syllable juncture?

Syllable junctures (or Sjs) occur within multisyllabic words. Sometimes it's easier to spell a word if you break it into meaningful parts. Syllables are meaningful parts that you might want to use.

BRAIN TICKLERS
Set #54 Combine Two Patterns to Form Multisyllabic Words

Now try combining syllable patterns from Set #53 to form multisyllabic words. How many words can you make?

(Answers are on page 186.)

BRAIN TICKLERS
Set #55 Find Syllable Patterns
in Long Words

Since many words have more than one
syllable, the patterns get more complex.

1. Write down ten words that have more
   than eight letters.

2. Find their consonant/vowel letter patterns.

3. Say the words aloud. Write down how
   many syllables each word has.

4. Write about any conclusions you can draw about where
   syllable junctures occur and about patterns of vowels and
   consonants.

(Answers are on page 186.)

Why . . . it
wouldn't be the
same without
Syllable Juncture!

Adding affixes

When we add word parts to the beginning or end of words, we also create syllable junctures. Let me tell you about some of the vocabulary we'll be using as we explore Sjs.

base: a word element to which affixes or other bases can be added. It may be a word in itself

<pre>
logical   +   il-   =   illogical
  base   prefix   (new word)
(word)

kempt   +   un-   =   unkempt
  base   prefix   (word)
(not word)
</pre>

Sometimes these word elements—whether they can stand alone or not—are called *roots*, *root words*, or *stems*.

gender: a word's reference to whether its subject is male (like *he*) or female (like *she*). Although they are used less often today, some nouns for occupations traditionally have had both a male and female form (actor/actress; waiter/waitress).

morpheme: the smallest unit of language that has meaning and cannot be subdivided. It can be a base word, like *compute*; a root, like *geo*; a prefix like *anti-*; or a suffix like *-s*.

plural: the form of a noun that indicates more than one. Plurals are formed in several ways.

Singular	Plural	Change Made
pig	pigs	+s
mouse	mice	internal change
fish	fish	no change

Plurals are discussed in more detail beginning on page 161.

prefix: an affix that is attached before a base.

root: see **base**.

suffix: an affix that is attached to the end of a base. A suffix can change the part of speech of the base (for example, noun to adjective: *beauty* → *beautiful*), change the tense (for example, present to past: *sniff* → *sniffed*), change the gender (*steward* → *stewardess*), or change the number (*pig* → *pigs*).

tense: the indication in a verb of whether it refers to the past, the present, or the future. There are regular and irregular verbs, which change in different ways to create tense.

	Present	Past	Present Perfect
Irregular	sing	sang	has sung
Regular	giggle	giggled	has giggled

BRAIN TICKLERS
Set #56 Brainstorm Occupation Words

Brainstorm as many occupation words that show gender as you can. If there is a form that is not gender-specific, give that also.

(Answers are on page 187.)

Double or nothing

When we change the form of a verb, adjective, or noun by adding a suffix, this is called *inflection*. We change verbs by adding endings such as *-s*, *-es*, *-ed*, *-en*, and *-ing*, and adjectives by adding endings such as *-er* and *-est*.

   (We'll talk about plurals in the next section.)

BRAIN TICKLERS
Set #57 Categorize Based on
Word Inflection

Look at and say each pair of words. Use patterns you see and hear to form groups, and write a rule for each group.

big	→	bigger	rat	→ ratted
flat	→	flattest	rate	→ rating
green	→	greener	steam	→ steaming
hop	→	hopping	stem	→ stemmed
hope	→	hoping	traffic	→ trafficked
hot	→	hotter	whip	→ whipping
panic	→	panicked	wipe	→ wiped
picnic	→	picnicking	young	→ younger
radio	→	radioed		

(Answers are on page 187.)

Some of the rules you discovered may look like these:

- doubling the consonant

→ Often a consonant following a "vowel" letter is doubled before adding a suffix to signal the reader that it is to be pronounced in its short form.

>*hop* → *hopped*, not *hoped*
>/hŏpt/ not /hōpt/

If the consonant is a *c* and it follows *i*, it will be "doubled" by adding *k*.

>*panic* → *panicked*, not *panicced*

- dropping the final *e*

→ Often the silent final e that signals a preceding long vowel is dropped before adding a suffix, because (a) the reader will interpret the vowel as long without it, and (b) its presence would affect the pronunciation of the suffix.

>*hope* → *hoped*, not *hopeed*
>/hōpt/ not /hō′pēd/

- changing *y* to *i*

→ Often y is changed to i before a suffix, because otherwise the y could be read as a consonant and change the pronunciation of the suffix.

>*happy* → *happier*, not *happyer*
>/hă′pēər/ not /hăp′yər/

Knowledge of how syllables fit together will help you become a better speller.

BRAIN TICKLERS
Set #58 Use Rules to Add Suffixes

Use the three rules for adding suffixes:

- doubling consonants
- dropping final *e*
- changing *y* to *i*
  to add the suffixes to these words.

1. bivouac + ing
2. zippy + er
3. fat + er
4. garlic + ed
5. funny + est
6. tip + ing
7. magic + ed
8. ally + ed
9. shellac + ing
10. sandy + er

11. cope + ing
12. clap + ing
13. angry + est
14. fate + ed
15. snag + ed
16. silly + er
17. slop + ed
18. havoc + ed
19. type + ing
20. slope + ed

(Answers are on page 188.)

PLURALS

Okay, we're going to take our first stab at Sjs (syllable junctures) while forming plurals of English words. This is tricky territory to navigate, because plurals are formed in different ways. Regular plurals are formed by adding -s or -es to words (*rat* → *rats* and *veto* → *vetoes*); and irregular plurals may have no change (*sheep* → *sheep*), changes in the middle of the word (*goose* → *geese*), or a host of other changes. Your best bet, if you're not sure, is to consult a dictionary.

Do-nothing plurals

This may turn out to be your favorite kind of plural. It's the kind where you look at the singular and . . . it's identical to the plural so you don't have to do a thing. Here's a list of words in which the singular equals the plural:

aircraft	humankind	samurai
alms	means	scissors
amends	moose	series
bellows	names of tribes and	shambles
chassis	races (Chinese)	sheep
deer	offspring	shrimp
fish	pants/slacks	species
forceps	proceeds	sweepstakes
goods	remains	swine
headquarters	rendezvous	United States

For American Indians/Native Americans, check with the tribe for its preferred use.

Easy street: regular plurals

This set of plurals follows two easy rules:

1. For most nouns in English, add -s to form the plural.

2. For nouns ending in *ch*, *s*, *sh*, *ss*, *tch*, *x*, *z*, or *zz*, form the plural by adding -es.

BRAIN TICKLERS
Set #59 Form Plurals for Words Ending in CH, S, SH, SS, TCH, X, Z, or ZZ

Write the plural for each of the singular nouns listed.

ax	buzz	glass
beach	church	guess
birch	crash	rush
box	dish	waltz
bus	dress	watch
bush	fox	

(Answers are on page 188.)

I say tomatoes, and you say potatoes

Besides whether to pronounce *tomato* as /tə mā' tō/ or /tə mŏ' tō/, another problem people have with *tomato* is how to render the plural. Here are tips for how to form plurals for words ending in *o*. Most words that end in Co (consonant, *o*) add *-es* to make the plural.

dingo → *dingoes*

Words that end in Vo (vowel, *o*) add *-s* to make the plural.

stereo → *stereos*

Musical terms that come from Italian words and end in Co also add *-s* to make the plural.

alto → *altos*

Here's a list:

Description	Instructions	Examples	
Consonant + *o*	Add *-es*	*echoes*	*vetoes*
		heroes	*potatoes*
		tomatoes	*lingoes*
Consonant + *o* (Musical Terms from Italian)	Add *-s*	*cellos* *pianos*	*solos* *sopranos*
Consonants + *o* (Oddball)	Add *-s*	*photos*	
Vowel + *o*	Add *-s*	*cameos*	*patios*
		radios	*ratios*
		rodeos	*taboos*

Choose your own plural

Here's another category you might like. For these nouns ending in *-o* you can choose your own plural. Yep, believe it or not, it doesn't matter whether you add *-s* or *-es* to these words. Either way is okay!

- carg**os** or carg**oes**
- banj**os** or banj**oes**
- grott**os** or grott**oes**
- hob**os** or hob**oes**
- tornad**os** or tornad**oes**
- mosquit**os** or mosquit**oes**
- volcan**os** or volcan**oes**

I can't decide!

AND this word takes the cake with three acceptable plural forms:

- buffal**os** or buffal**oes** OR buffal**o**—your choice.

Two different plurals—two different meanings

Some other words have two different plurals, but each plural has a different meaning. Here's a list for you..

Singular	Plural # 1 and Meaning	Plural # 2 and Meaning
brother	brothers (two boys born to the same parents)	brethren (members of the same society, e.g., the Quakers)
die	dies (tools used to stamp)	dice (numbered cubes used for games)
genius	geniuses (brilliant people)	genii (imaginary spirits, like the one in *Aladdin*)
index	indexes (lists of book contents)	indices (algebraic signs)
staff	staves (poles or supports; the five-line systems on which music is written)	staffs (groups of assistants)

What's the difference between a dwarf and an elf?

The difference is that you form the plural of *dwarf* by adding *-s* (*dwarfs*) or changing *f* to *v* and adding *-es* (dwarves) but the only plural of *elf* is (*elves*). Here are the rules:

+ s
or f → v + es   f → v + es

All words ending in *f* or *fe* form plurals in one of three patterns:

- *f* + *s*
- *fe* + *s*   — regular   • *f* → *v* + *es* — irregular

Examples of words ending in *f* or *fe* that form regular plurals

Regular Plurals of words ending in *f* or *fe*	Irregular Plurals of words ending in *f*	
chief → chiefs	calf → calves	self → selves
clef → clefs	elf → elves	sheaf → sheaves
proof → proofs	half → halves	shelf → shelves
reef → reefs	knife → knives	thief → thieves
waif → waifs	leaf → leaves	wife → wives
café → cafés	life → lives	wolf → wolves
safe → safes	loaf → loaves	

The four ODDBALLS in this group are *dwarf, wharf, scarf,* and *hoof.* For these four words, you can add either *-s* or change *f* to *v* and add *-es,* whichever you like. And, just for the record, words ending in a double *ff* (except *staff,* which has two plurals—see page 164—and *dandruff,* which isn't clearly singular or plural and has no plural form) all take the *-s* ending. For example:

sheriffs

tariffs

mastiffs

How wise are you . . .

. . . when it comes to making plural forms for nouns ending in -*y*? Here are the rules:

- If the noun ends in Vy (vowel, *y*) add -*s*.

    decoy → decoys

- If the noun ends in Cy (consonant, *y*) or a consonant sound and *y* (for example, in *colloquy*, in which the *qu* sounds like /kw/), change -*y* to -*i* and add -*es*.

    bunny → bunnies

BRAIN TICKLERS
Set #60 Form Plurals for Words Ending in Y

Write the plural for each noun listed below.

beauty	donkey	soliloquy
bunny	French fry	Sunday
buy	guy	tray
city	monkey	turkey

(Answers are on page 189.)

Why can't the Romans learn to pluralize?

Words of foreign origin can have unusual plurals, because although there may be a "regular" plural formed with -*s* or -*es*, the preferred plural may be from their original language. This chart will give you an idea of some of the Latin words in this group.

LATIN PLURALS		
Singular	**Rules**	**Plural**
alumnus cactus fungus nucleus radius	(us → i)	alumni cacti fungi nuclei radii
analysis basis crisis diagnosis hypothesis	(is → es)	analyses bases crises diagnoses hypotheses
bacterium datum medium ovum	(um → a)	bacteria data media ova
alumna antenna (insect feelers) larva vertebra	(a → ae)	alumnae antennae larvae vertebrae
matrix	(ix → ices)	matrices
criterion	(on → a)	criteria

BRAIN TICKLERS
Set #61 Form Plurals for Words from Latin

Use the patterns in the Latin plurals chart to
form the plurals of the following words:

antithesis	oasis	referendum
dictum	optimum	serum
focus	parenthesis	streptococcus
gladiolus	phenomenon	ulna
memorandum		

(Answers are on page 189.)

Major renovations: inside-out plurals

These are the words that change in the middle, rather than at the
end.

Singular	Plural	Singular	Plural
child	children	mouse	mice
foot	feet	man	men
goose	geese	woman	women
tooth	teeth	ox	oxen
louse	lice	person	people

Which word takes the *s*?: plurals of compound words

Simple—usually you just pick the main noun and form its plural as you would if it stood alone. So:

- attorney-at-law → attorneys-at-law
- bachelor's degree → bachelor's degrees
- man-of-war → men-of-war
- mother-in-law → mothers-in-law
- passer-by → passers-by
- runner-up → runners-up
- step-child → step-children

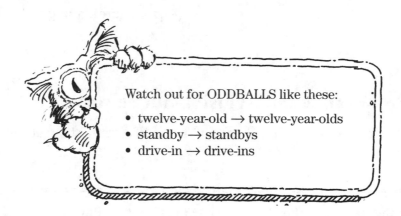

Watch out for ODDBALLS like these:

- twelve-year-old → twelve-year-olds
- standby → standbys
- drive-in → drive-ins

Plurals of proper names: Podhaizers, Yendrzeskis, Nguyens, and Dinwiddies

This is so simple that some people think it's complicated. Here's the rule:

If a proper noun ends in *ch*, *s*, *sh*, *ss*, *tch*, *x*, *z* or *zz* in the singular, add *-es*. Otherwise, just add *-s*, even if the word ends in Cy (consonant, *y*).

Singular	Plural
Adonis	Adonises
Denny	Dennys
Szymkowicz	Szymkowiczes
Choothamkhajorn	Choothamkhajorns
Lichty-Marcoux	Lichty-Marcouxes

Plurals of letters, dates, numbers, symbols, and abbreviations

Easy . . . for letters, dates, numbers, and symbols, just stick on an apostrophe and -s, like this:

Singular	Plural
x	x's
1990 (the year)	1990's
&	&'s
3	3's

Don't confuse these plurals with possessives.

For an abbreviation with periods, add an apostrophe and -s. If it has no periods, just add -s:

YMCA → YMCAs
Ph.D. → Ph.D.'s
Co. → → Co.'s

For more about abbreviations, see page 142.

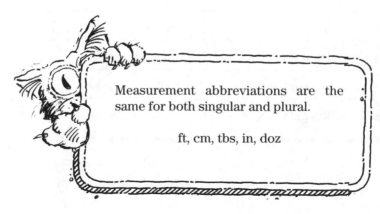

Measurement abbreviations are the same for both singular and plural.

ft, cm, tbs, in, doz

SIMPLE PREFIXES

Philosopher Gregory Bateson in the essay "Every Schoolboy Knows" states some presuppositions that he thinks important, one of them being:

> The Division of the Perceived Universe into Parts and Whole is Convenient and May Be Necessary, . . . But No Necessity Determines How It Shall Be Done.

Sometimes textbooks do a disservice by slicing things only one way. Looking at the same object of study from multiple perspectives may give you a greater understanding. So we're going to call this:

Slicing and dicing

We can talk about prefixes in a number of different ways.

If we talk about their:	we can gain insight into:
etymological source	the words they would likely be combined with: generally words from the same language
part of speech	the kind of word they will be attached to: generally words acting as specific parts of speech
meaning	how to use them

So we could talk about Greek prefixes (etymology); prefixes that are prepositional, adjectival, and adverbial (part of speech); or the prefixes *micro-* and *mini-*, which both mean small (meaning). Or we could just list them all alphabetically.

BRAIN TICKLERS
Set #62 Categorize Prefixes

Study this list of 47 prefixes (we'll deal with a special group called "assimilated prefixes" later). Group them using one of the categories on the left side of the chart on page 173: language of origin, part of speech of the word they attach to, or related meanings. You may find a dictionary helpful for this. Write a sentence or two about how you organized the prefixes.

a-	without, not
a-	on, in
a-	up, out, away
amphi-	around, both
anti-*	against, opposite
auto-	self
be-	around, about, away, thoroughly
bi-	two, twice
cata-**	down, away, against
circum-	around, on all sides
contra-	against
counter-	opposite
de-	reversal, removal, away, from, off, down
dia-	through, together
equi-	equal
eu-	good, pleasant
extra-	beyond, outside
hemi-	half

*When *anti-* precedes a base word starting with a "vowel" letter, you usually add a hyphen, as in *anti-American*. But for the word *antacid*, you drop the *i*.

**Another oddball is *cata-* in the word *category*—it loses its final *a*.

hyper-	extra, over, excessive, beyond
hypo-	under, beneath, below
inter-	among, between
intra-	within
macro-	large
mal-	bad, wrongful
micro-	very small
mis-	wrongly, badly, not correct
multi-	many
neo-	new
non-	against, not, without
out-	to a greater degree, located externally or outside
over-	over, excessively
para-	beside, similar to, beyond
peri-	about, around
post-	after, following
pre-	before
pro-	forward, in place of, favoring
pseudo-	false, pretended, not real
re-	again, back, backward
retro-	back, backward
semi-	half, twice
super-	above, extra, over
trans-	across, beyond
tri-	three, every third
ultra-	beyond, excessively
un-	not, opposing
under-	below, beneath
uni-	one

Here's a sample of how you might set up your paper do this exercise:

Language of Origin		
Old English	**Greek**	**Latin**

(Answers are on page 189.)

BRAIN TICKLERS
Set #63 Identify Words
That Have Specific Prefixes

1. Choose fifteen prefixes on the list. Think of at least two words that have each prefix. Some will be easy, others more complicated. Keep a list.

2. Which word or root or base can you find that works with the greatest number of these prefixes?

(Answers are on page 190.)

BRAIN TICKLERS
Set #64 Make Your Own Spelling Rules

Using the words you've collected in Set #63, make up a list of spelling rules that would help you in the future. Give example words to demonstrate each rule.

(Answers are on page 194.)

SIMPLE SUFFIXES

America's most wanted

What suffix do you think is most used? I haven't found any statistics about this, but if *-ed* isn't the most frequently used suffix, it's certainly up there. Let's take a look at *-ed* and its sound.

BRAIN TICKLERS
Set #65 Supply Past Tense for Verbs

Write the past tense for each verb listed.
What visual patterns do you notice?

bat	fight	pot
bide	grade	press
boil	graze	rest
catch	greet	sail
dare	hop	sleep
deal	kneel	slop
dial	lace	snag
fix	lend	track
flap	lie	

(Answers are on page 194.)

BRAIN TICKLERS
Set #66 Find Rhyming Verbs with Matching Past Tense

For each word in Set #65, see if you can find
a rhyme word that forms its past tense in the
same way. Then, if you can, write another
rhyme word that forms its past tense in a different way. Write a sentence or two about your
findings.

(Answers are on page 195.)

BRAIN TICKLERS
Set #67 Find Sound Patterns
in Rhyming Verbs

Review your answers to Set #65, this time searching for sound patterns. Use the sound patterns you find in the endings to group the words.

(Answers are on page 196.)

BRAIN TICKLERS
Set #68 Add -ED and -ING Suffixes

Three different things can happen to the end of a base or root when an *-ed* or *-ing* ending is added. Add both suffixes to each word below, and sort the results into three groups depending on how you treated the base word.

bump   fit   grate   hop   hope   laugh
rain   rub   tickle

(Answers are on page 196.)

Suffix survey

Slicing, dicing, mincing, chopping, and blending

We could talk about suffixes in even more different ways than
we had for prefixes.

If we talk about their:	we can gain insight into:
etymological source	the base words they would likely be combined with (generally words from the same language)
forms	how to attach them to the base words or word parts they combine with
meaning	how to use them
function	the effect they have on the base word they are attached to (e.g., turning a verb into a noun)

So we could talk about Latin suffixes (etymology); the suffix /sh°ŋ/ and its various spellings (forms); suffixes that tell where a person is from, like -*er* and -*ian* (meaning); or how the suffix -*tion* can turn the verb *civilize* into the noun *civilization* (function). Or we could just list them all alphabetically.

Let's start with the **function** of making an adverb. Besides past tense suffixes and plurals, the adverbial suffix -*ly* is probably one of the most common suffixes. Some things adverbs with -*ly* endings can do are tell

- how (helplessly),
- to what extent (frequently),
- how much (slightly), and
- when (weekly).

This is how you add the endings to adjectives or nouns to make adverbs:

Word Ending	Change to Make Adverb	Samples
y	change *y* to *i* and add -*ly*	clumsy → clumsily; happy → happily
le	drop *le* and add -*ly*	gentle → gently; simple → simply
ll	drop one *l* and add -*ly*	dull → dully; full → fully

Suf-fixation

Now let's talk about the **function** of making a noun. How many suffixes do you think there are that indicate nouns? There are at least ninety! Ninety is too many to discuss at once, so let's narrow it down to some subcategories.

BRAIN TICKLERS
Set #69 Make Proper Adjectives

1. For each name of a PLACE listed below, write a sentence based on the model below in which you substitute the country name and add a suffix to form the noun that names a person who comes from that place. Use this model:

    A person who comes from the Americas is an _____.

    Be careful, because not all of these nouns are formed with the same suffix.

(Use a dictionary if necessary.) Make a list of the different suffixes you used.

Nigeria   Iraq   Hungary   Panama   Vermont   Japan

2. When you add a suffix to make most nouns, as in all the cases we've discussed, there are four possibilities:
    * simply add the suffix with no other change
    * double the final consonant and add the suffix
    * drop the final *e* and add the suffix (somtimes a letter before the *e* is dropped, too)
    * change *y* to *i* and add the suffix

But with place names, there can be different kinds of changes. Look at these groups of proper adjectives. What was done to the name of each place before the suffix was added?

* Swedish   Finnish   Polish   Turkish   English   Irish   Spanish

* Canadian   Peruvian   Chilean   Mexican   Italian   Jordanian

* Chinese   Balinese   Javanese   Vietnamese   Taiwanese

* Bengali   Israeli   Kuwaiti   Saudi

(Answers are on page 196.)

BRAIN TICKLERS
Set #70 Form Occupation Words

Here are some suffixes that form words that tell what PEOPLE do, activities they are involved in, their vocations, or their hobbies. For each suffix, write at least one word that has that suffix. What changes did you make as you added the suffixes?

-aire	-eer	-ian
-ant	-ent	-ist
-ee	-er	-or

(Answers are on page 197.)

BRAIN TICKLERS
Set #71 Noun Suffix Puzzle

The noun suffixes listed below have to do with ideas, characteristics, attitudes, beliefs, and feelings—all ABSTRACT concepts. Read the definition and the sample word for each suffix.

1. What changes occurred in the base words as the suffixes were added?

2. Put the red words into the puzzle.

-ation state, condition, or quality of   isolate → isolation

-cy a quality or condition   dependence → dependency

-dom the condition of being ___   free → freedom

-hood state, condition, or quality of being   brother → brotherhood

-ics the science or art of   ethos → ethics

-ism a doctrine or system or principle   Buddha → Buddhism

-ment action or state   judge → judgment

-ness state, quality, or condition of being   kind → kindness

-red the condition of   hate → hatred

-ship quality or condition of   friend → friendship

-tude a condition or state of being   gratis → gratitude

-ty, ity a condition or quality   animus → animosity

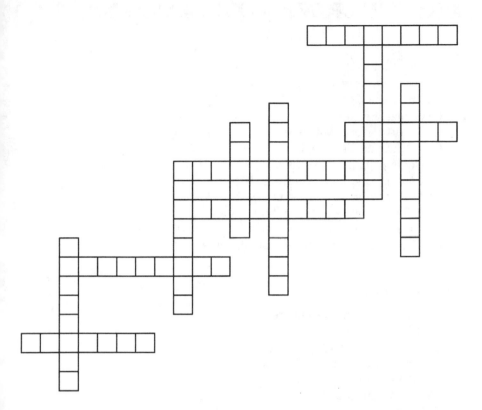

(Answers are on page 197.)

BRAIN TICKLERS—THE ANSWERS

Set #53, page 154

Answers will vary. Possible responses:
CV: my, he, no, go, we
CVC: pig, hog, pen, cob, mud
CCV: sty, she, cry, two, gnu
CVV: May, hue, lie, boo, key
CVCe: hope, pure, love, give, vale
CVCC: sign, mold, park, warm, Turk
CCVC: know, stem, Kris, shut, Fred
CVVC: jail, boat, been, pour, boil
CCVV: free, blue, thou, flea, whoa
CVCCE: purse, horse, tense, range, bathe

Set #54, page 154

Answers will vary. Possible responses:
CV CV   mama
CVC CVC   market
CVC CVV   coffee
CV CVVC   reboot
CVV CVV   mayday
CVV CVC   Dayton
CVC CV   manly
and so on

Set #55, page 155

Possible responses:
1, 2, and 3:
unanimous: VCVCVCVVC; 4 syllables
imagination: VCVCVCVCVVC; 5 syllables
understanding: VCCVCCCVCCVCC; 4 syllables
calliopes: CVCCVVCVC; 4 syllables
innovation: VCCVCVCVVC; 4 syllables
independent: VCCVCVCCVCC; 4 syllables
cauliflower: CVVCVCCVCVC; 4 syllables
melancholy: CVCVCCCVCV; 4 syllables
farsighted: CVCCVCCCVC; 3 syllables
optimistic: VCCVCVCCVC; 4 syllables

4. Answers will vary. Observations on words shown:
   Vowels tend to appear singly (34 times), but occasionally can be found in groups of two (4 times), whereas consonants come in groups of two (12 times) and groups of three (3 times) and also appear singly (27 times).

   Often the sound of the word splits between the double or within the triple consonants. Syllables with short vowels seem to often both begin and end with consonants. Syllables with long vowels seem to end with the vowel.

Set #56, page 158

Possible responses:

Male Form	Female Form	Non-Specific Form
businessman	businesswoman	business person
chairman	chairwoman	chair
cowboy	cowgirl	cowhand
farmer	farmerette	farmer
fireman		fire fighter
garbage man		sanitation worker
mailman; postman		mail carrier; postal worker
shepherd	shepherdess	shepherd
steward	stewardess	flight attendant
usher	usherette	usher

Set #57, page 158

1. If you are adding -ed or -ing to a word ending in -ic, double the consonant by adding a k.

   panic   panicked
   picnic   picnicking
   traffic   trafficked

2. If you are adding an ending to a word with a short vowel followed by a single consonant, double that consonant.

hop	hopping	big	bigger
rat	ratted	flat	flattest
stem	stemmed	hot	hotter
whip	whipping		

3. If you are adding an ending to a word with a short vowel already followed by two consonants, simply add the ending.

young younger

4. If you are adding an ending to a word with a long vowel, simply add the ending, or if the word ends in silent -e, drop the e and add the ending.

hope	hoping	steam	steaming
radio	radioed	wipe	wiped
rate	rating	green	greener

Set #58, page 160

1. bivouacking
2. zippier
3. fatter
4. garlicked
5. funniest
6. tipping
7. magicked
8. allied
9. shellacking
10. sandier
11. coping
12. clapping
13. angriest
14. fated
15. snagged
16. sillier
17. slopped
18. havocked
19. typing
20. sloped

Set #59, page 162

axes
beaches
birches
boxes
buses
bushes

buzzes
churches
crashes
dishes
dresses
foxes

glasses
guesses
rushes
waltzes
watches

Set #60, page 167

beauties	donkeys	soliloquies
bunnies	French fries	Sundays
buys	guys	trays
cities	monkeys	turkeys

Set #61, page 169

antitheses	oases	referenda
dicta	optima	sera
foci	parentheses	streptococci
gladioli	phenomena	ulnae
memoranda		

Set #62, page 174

Possible responses: I grouped the prefixes by language of origin:

Old English

a- on, in
a- up, out, away
be- around, about, away, thoroughly
mis- wrongly, badly, not correct

out- to a greater degree, located externally or outside
over- over, excessively
un- not, opposing

Greek

a- without, not
amphi- around, both
anti- against, opposite
auto- self
bi- two, twice
cata- down, away, against
dia- through, together
eu- good, pleasant
hemi- half

hyper- extra, over, excessive, beyond
hypo- under, beneath, below
macro- large
micro- very small
neo- new
para- beside, similar to, beyond
peri- about, around
pseudo- false, pretended, not real

Latin

circum- around, on all sides
contra- against
counter- opposite
de- reversal, removal, away, from, off, down
equi- equal
extra- beyond, outside
inter- among, between
intra- within
mal- bad, wrongful
multi- many
non- against, not, without
post- after, following

pre- before
pro- forward, in place of, favoring
re- again, back, backward
retro- back, backward
semi- half, twice
super- above, extra, over
trans- across, beyond
tri- three, every third
ultra- beyond, excessively
under- below, beneath
uni- one

Set #63, page 176

1. Possible responses:

Old English		
Prefix	**Meaning**	**Examples**
a-	on, in	abed, aboard, afoot, asleep
a-	up, out, away	arise, awake
be-	around, about, away, thoroughly	behead, beloved, beset
mis-	wrongly, badly, not correct	misapply, misinterpret, mismanage, misspell, mistake
out-	to a greater degree, located externally or outside	outboard, outdo, outhouse, outlive, outshine, outshoot
over-	over, excessively	overcompensate, overdrive, overdue, overrun, oversee
un-	not, opposing	unaccompanied, undo, unhappy, unlock, untrue

Greek		
Prefix	**Meaning**	**Examples**
a-	without, not	amoral, apolitical
amphi-	around, both	amphibious amphitheater
anti-	against, opposite	antibody, antiseptic, antipathy
auto-	self	autobiography, automobile
bi-	two, twice	bicycle, bimonthly
cata-	down, away, against	cataclysm, catastrophe
dia-	through, together	dialogue, diameter
eu-	good, pleasant	eulogy, euphemism
hemi-	half	hemiplegic, hemisphere
hyper-	extra, over, excessive, beyond	hypercritical, hypertension, hyperthermia
hypo-	under, beneath, below	hypocritical, hypodermic, hypothesis
macro-	large	macrobiotic, macrocosm
micro-	very small	microcosm, micromanage, microscope
neo-	new	neolithic, neologism, neonatal, neo-Nazi
para-	beside, similar to, beyond	paragraph, paranormal, paraphrase, paraprofessional
peri-	about, around	perimeter, periscope
pseudo-	false, pretended, not real	pseudonym, pseudopod, pseudoscience

Latin		
Prefix	**Meaning**	**Examples**
circum-	around, on all sides	circumference, circumnavigate
contra-	against	contradict, contraindicated
counter-	opposite	counteract, counterrevolution
de-	reversal, removal, away, from, off, down	deactivate, decapitate, decode, decrease, delouse, demean, destroy
equi-	equal	equidistant, equilateral, equivalent
extra-	beyond, outside	extracurricular, extraordinary, extraterrestrial
inter-	among, between	intermurals, international, interplanetary, interstate
intra-	within	intramurals, intramuscular, intravenous
mal-	bad, wrongful	malalignment, malignant, malodorous, maltreatment
multi-	many	multicolored, multiform, multimillionaire, multinational
non-	against, not, without	nonentity, nonessential, nonexistent, nonsense, nonstop, nonviolence
post-	after, following	postdate, postgraduate, postpone, postscript

Prefix	Meaning	Examples
pre-	before	preclude, prefix, preheat, prejudge
pro-	forward, in place of, favoring	proclaim, prolong, pronoun, prorevolution
re-	again, back, backward	reappear, relinquish, repair, repay, replace
retro-	back, backward	retroactive, retrorocket, retrospect
semi-	half, twice	semiannual, semicircular, semidetached, semiformal
super-	above, extra, over	supernatural, supersaturated, superscript, superstar
trans-	across, beyond	transcontinental, transpolar, transport
tri-	three, every third	triangle, tricycle, trimonthly
ultra-	beyond, excessively	ultraconservative, ultramodern, ultrasonic, ultraviolet
under-	below, beneath	underground, underhanded, underwater, underwear
uni-	one	unicycle, unison

2. Possible responses:

active: counteractive, hyperactive, interactive, overactive, proactive, reactive, retroactive, semiactive

do: outdo, overdo, undo

cycle: bicycle, tricycle, recycle, unicycle

critical: diacritical, hypercritical, uncritical

form: deform, malform, microform, reform, uniform

logue: catalogue, dialogue, prologue

monthly: bimonthly, trimonthly, semimonthly

vert: controvert, extrovert (or extravert), revert

verse: converse, reverse, transverse, universe

scribe: circumscribe, describe, proscribe, transcribe

script: postscript, prescript, superscript, transcript

spect: circumspect, prospect, respect, retrospect

Set #64, page 176

Possible responses:

1. When adding a prefix to a base that begins with the same letter the prefix ends with, you will have a double letter: *misspell, overrun, counterrevolution*

2. When adding a prefix that ends in a vowel letter to a base that begins with a vowel letter, you will have a double vowel letter: *contraindicated, deactivate, extraordinary, reappear, retroactive, semiannual, triangle*

3. When adding a prefix to a base that begins with a capital letter, use a hyphen and keep the capital letter capitalized: *anti-American, neo-Nazi*

4. In almost every case, the prefix is spelled exactly the same way, no matter what base it is added to: *deactivate, decapitate, decode, decrease, delouse, demand, destroy,* and so on.

Set #65, page 178

End in -ed

batted	graded	pressed
bided/bode	grazed	rested
boiled	greeted	sailed
dared	hopped	slopped
dialed	laced	snagged
fixed	lied	tracked
flapped	potted	

End in -t

caught	fought	lent
dealt	knelt	slept

Set #66, page 178

Original Word	Rhyme Word w. Matching Past Tense	Rhyme Word w. Different Past Tense
bat–batted	pat–patted	
bide–bided	side–sided	
bide–bode	ride–rode	
boil–boiled	toil–toiled	
catch–caught	—	match–matched
dare–dared	scare–scared	
deal–dealt	—	seal–sealed; steal–stole
dial–dialed		
fix–fixed	mix–mixed	
flap–flapped	trap–trapped	
fight–fought		sight–sighted; light–lit
grade–graded	fade–faded	
graze–grazed	haze–hazed	
greet–greeted	sheet–sheeted	meet–met
hop–hopped	stop–stopped	
kneel–knelt	feel–felt	peel–peeled
lace–laced	face–faced	
lend–lent	bend–bent	mend–mended
lie–lied	die–died	
pot–potted	spot–spotted	
press–pressed	bless–blessed	
rest–rested	best–bested	
sail–sailed	mail–mailed	
sleep–slept	keep–kept	bleep–bleeped
slop–slopped	drop–dropped	
snag–snagged	tag–tagged	
track–tracked	snack–snacked	

Set #67, page 179

Past tenses ending in -*ed* with the sound /t/:

fixed	laced	slopped
flapped	pressed	tracked
hopped		

Past tenses ending in -*ed* with the sounds /d/:

batted	greeted	rested
bided	potted	
graded		

Past tenses that end in -*ed* and have the sound /d/:

boiled	dialed	sailed
bode	grazed	snagged
dared	lied	

Past tenses ending in -*t* that end with the sound /t/:

caught	fought	lent
dealt	knelt	slept

Set #68, page 179

no change	**double final consonant**	**drop final *e***
bumped, bumping	fitted, fitting	grated, grating
laughed, laughing	hopped, hopping	hoped, hoping
rained, raining	rubbed, rubbing	tickled, tickling

Set #69, page 182

1.
Nigerian	Iraqi	Hungarian	Panamanian	Vermonter	Japanese
-*n*	-*i*	*y* to *i+an*	-*nian*	-*er*	-*ese*

2.

Sweden → Swedish Turkey → Turkish Spain → Spanish	Finland → Finnish England → English	Poland → Polish Ireland → Irish
Canada → Canadian Mexico → Mexican	Peru → Peruvian Italy → Italian	Chile → Chilean Jordan → Jordanian
China → Chinese Vietnam → Vietnamese	Bali → Balinese Taiwan → Taiwanese	Java → Javanese
Bengal → Bengali Israel → Israeli	Kuwait → Kuwaiti	Saudi → Saudi

None of these groups can be explained by a single rule. The first two are very complicated groups.

Set #70, page 183

Possible responses:

SUFFIX	WORDS THAT INCLUDE THE SUFFIX		
-aire*	commissionaire	legionnaire	millionaire
-ant	debutant	assistant	descendant
-ee	referee	employee	appointee
-eer	engineer	auctioneer	rocketeer
-ent	student	correspondent	superintendent
-er	farmer	reporter	dancer
-ian	physician	musician	phonetician
-ist	typist	novelist	pianist
-or	actor	aviator	investigator

*"These words come from French. . . ."

Set #71, pages 184–185

1. **drop the *e*:** isolate; dependence; judge; hate
   no change: free; brother; kind; friend
   drop the -*os*: ethos
   drop the -*a*: Buddhism
   drop the -*s*: gratis
   drop the -*us*: animus

2.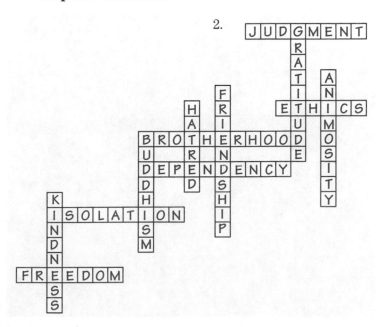

Part Four

DERIVATIONAL CONSISTENCY

Derivation tells us where something comes from.
It's the same idea as etymology.
When we trace the derivation of a word,
we learn about the language in which it originated
and how it came into English. In this section we
will work toward understanding how a word's
appearance can give us clues that help us
understand meaning or sound.

CHAPTER EIGHT

More About Suffixes

CHANGES IN SOUND

Pastry shop: what's under the crust?

Whether you prefer pie, calzone, ravioli, doughnuts, or pierogi, if you've ever bought a closed pastry you may have experienced that moment of doubt—it looks like all the others, but what's really inside? All the pastries look the same, but are they the same? There are some words like those pastries—words that look somewhat alike, but aren't pronounced alike. Fortunately,

They look alike but have different fillings.

these words follow some rules of pronunciation, so they are identifiable.

Here's an example. Look at these words:

sign	signal
signed	signatory
signer	signature
signing	

All the words have the letters **s-i-g-n** in them. They look like they should all be pronounced in a similar way, but if you try saying them, you'll see that they're not. The letters stay the same to help you understand that the words have related meanings. But watch out when you spell them! Sometimes you hear the /g/ sound, and sometimes you don't, but you always have to write the letter *g*. Do you remember the term **inert letter** from Chapter 5? **Inert letters** is the name for letters that appear in a word segment to help you recognize the meaning, even though they aren't heard. The *g*'s that you don't hear but have to write are inert letters.

This may seem complicated or frustrating because you have to write letters that you don't hear when you say the word. But that *g* is actually useful. Here's why: Say there wasn't a *g* in the word *sign*. Then you'd spell it *s-i-n*, right? Now the complications are even greater. Is the word *sin*, /sĭn/ meaning "an offense against God" or *sin*, /sīn/ the abbreviation in trigonometry for *sine*, or sin /sēn/, as some people pronounce the twenty-first letter of the Hebrew alphabet, or is it *si[g]n* /sīn/?

You may remember that the word **morpheme** names a unit of language, like *sign*, that has a stable meaning and cannot be divided into smaller parts. It is kind of like a molecule, which is the smallest possible example of a compound.
The word *pig* is a single morpheme.
Piglet has two morphemes: *pig* and the diminutive suffix *-let*.
Pigheaded has three: *pig* and *head* and *-ed*, a suffix which makes it an adjective.
Pigheadedness has four, including *-ness*, a suffix meaning "a state or quality of being."

English tries to keep a single spelling for a single morpheme, even when the pronunciation changes. The different pronunciations of the same morphenes are called **alternations**.

BRAIN TICKLERS
Set #72 Identify Silent Letters

For each set of words in the following list, identify the letter that is silent in one or some words and sounded in the other(s).

assign, assignation
condemn, condemnation
soft, soften, softly
economical, economically /ĕk′ ə-nŏ m′ ĭ -klē /

Reminder: The ə represents the schwa sound—the unaccented sound that is voiced like short *u*.

debt, debit
doubt, dubious
grand, grandma /grăm′ mä′/
hand, handsome, handkerchief

(Answers are on page 224.)

Everybody SH!

There are other situations in which words sound different but are obviously connected in meaning and spelling. One case is when suffixes pronounced /ən/ are added to words that end in *ic* or *t*. Once you add that ending, the *c* or *t* no longer sounds like itself, but assumes a /sh/ sound. For example, we say *connect* with a /t/ at the end, but in *connection*, we hear /sh/ and no /t/.

In British English, they change the spelling to show this: *connexion*.

The easy part for spelling is that these words just add *-ion* or *-ian* at the end, keeping their same last letter, as in

connect → connection or *physic → physician.*

Or, if they end in *-te*, they drop the *e* and add *-ion* as in

delete → deletion.

BRAIN TICKLERS
Set #73 Add -ION and -IAN Suffixes

Add an *-ion* or *-ian* ending to each word below. Underline the letter that is seen but not heard.

academic	considerate	invent
adopt	contort	logistic
assert	demonstrate	magic
associate	discriminate	music
attract	electric	pediatric
circulate	except	politic
clinic	inhibit	reflect
complete	inspect	select
composite	instruct	statistic

We'll talk more about *-ion* and *-ian* endings later.

(Answers are on page 225.)

Shorting out

In "Everybody SH!" you saw that sometimes spelling doesn't reflect the pronunciation changes that occur at the final syllable juncture when you add a suffix to a word. In the cases we looked at, there was a change in the pronunciation of the final consonant sound in the base.

In some words, there is a change in the pronunciation of a vowel in a particular syllable, although the spelling in that syllable stays the same. In one group of words, a schwa pronunciation changes to a short vowel pronunciation with the addition of a suffix. Remember that schwa has the sound of short *u* in an unaccented syllable. Let's look at how the schwa-to-short vowel change works.

Take the words *local* and *legal*. They are each accented on the first syllable, which is pronounced with a long vowel:

local   /lō′kəl/   legəl   /lē′gəl/

The vowel in the second syllable is a schwa. Listen to what happens when you add the ending *-ity*. The accented syllable changes to the second syllable.

locality   /lō-kăl′ ĭ-tē/   legality   /lē-găl′ ĭ-tē/

Because schwa exists only in UNaccented syllables, the sound of the second syllable CAN'T be schwa anymore, so the sound returns to the short vowel /ă/. But the spelling doesn't change.

BRAIN TICKLERS
Set #74 Identify Accented Syllables in Words with Suffixes I

Notice how you can add the suffix indicated to each base word. Underline the accented syllable in the resulting word. Identify the vowel sound you hear in that syllable.

central + -ity = centrality
economy + -ics = economics
formal + -ity = formality
metal + -ic = metallic
relative + -ity = relativity

(Answers are on page 225.)

Shorting out two

Under certain circumstances, adding a suffix can change the pronunciation of a long vowel to a short vowel—again, without a spelling change.

Take the word *please*. It has a long vowel sound in the single, accented syllable:

please   /plēz/

Listen to what happens when you add the ending sound -*ant*. The accented syllable stays the same, but the long vowel sound becomes short:

pleasant   /plĕz′ənt/

BRAIN TICKLERS
Set #75 Identify Accented Syllables in Words with Suffixes II

Notice how you can add the suffix indicated to each base word with a long vowel sound in the accented syllable. Underline the accented syllable in the resulting word. Identify the vowel sound you hear in that syllable.

bile + -ious = bilious
cone + -ic = conic
crime + -inal = criminal
diabetes + -ic = diabetic

divine + -ity = divinity
mime + -ic = mimic
sane + -ity = sanity
serene + -ity = serenity

state + -ic = static
tone + -ic = tonic
volcano + -ic = volcanic

(Answers are on page 225.)

All things being equal

Do you remember that the word *schwa* comes from a Syriac word meaning "equal"—maybe because many different sounds are kind of "equalized" into one sound (more or less) in unstressed syllables? When you add a suffix to a base word, and the accentuation of the word changes so that a syllable that was stressed is no longer stressed, a vowel with a long pronunciation can end up being pronounced as a schwa. The spelling stays the same so that you can recognize that the words are related, but the sound changes.

Take the word *compose*. It has a long vowel sound in the second syllable, which is stressed:

• compose   /kəm-pōz′/

Listen to what happens when you add the ending *-ition*. The accented syllable changes, and the long vowel sound becomes a schwa:

• composition   /kŏm′pə-zĭ sh′ən/

BRAIN TICKLERS
Set #76 Identify Accented Syllables in Words with Suffixes III

Notice how you can add the suffix indicated to each base word. Underline the accented syllable in the resulting word. Identify the change in vowel sound that occurred. What do all the base words have in common? Add two of your own.

admire + -ation = admiration   preside + -ent = president
coincide + -ent = coincident   reside + -ent = resident
define + -ition = definition

(Answers are on page 225.)

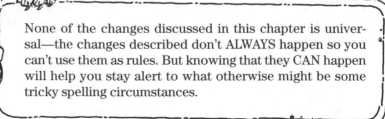

None of the changes discussed in this chapter is universal—the changes described don't ALWAYS happen so you can't use them as rules. But knowing that they CAN happen will help you stay alert to what otherwise might be some tricky spelling circumstances.

SAME SOUND, DIFFERENT LOOK

Did you ever notice that many suffixes with identical sounds are spelled different ways? In this section we will sort out some of these homophonic suffixes so that you can understand them better.

Pay attenssion! I mean, pay attencian! Oh, just pay attention!

There are two ways of beginning to sort out the / n/ endings in order to make sense of them: one is by sight, and the other is by sound. We will try both. To begin with, you should know that the following suffixes are in this group:

-sion   *-ssion*   *-tion*   *-ician*   *-en*

Oh,
just pay
atten/shən/.

BRAIN TICKLERS
Set #77 Add -ION Suffixes and Classify Results

Look at this chart. It has three groups and 10 subgroups.

Group 1: Words That Take the *–sion* Ending			
a. decide	evade	erode	conclude

Group 2: Words That Take the *–tion* Ending			
a. compose	expose	suppose	transpose
b. civilize	realize	specialize	capitalize
c. relax	tax	vex	fix
d. document	indent	lament	plant

Group 3: Words That Take the *–ion* Ending			
a. express	regress	possess	impress
b. agitate	complicate	concentrate	educate
c. confuse	imprecise	televise	profuse
d. constitute	contribute	pollute	substitute
e. act	reflect	predict	instruct

Working through the chart in order, take the lettered subgroups one at a time. Look at each base word.

1. Write the word made by adding the suffix that's identified in the group name. As you add the suffix, make note of the changes you made to the base word.

2. Regroup the words based on the steps you took to add the designated suffix, writing the "rule" for each new group you've created.

(Answers are on page 226.)

Sound it out

Another approach to /ən/ words focuses on sound and meaning. *-ician* and *-en* are meaning groups as well as visual groups:

-ician makes a noun that identifies a person's profession or practice.

magic → magician   "someone skilled in magic"
diet → dietician   "someone qualified to give diet advice"

This suffix *-en* creates a verb concerned with a meaning related to causing or becoming from an adjective:

cheap → cheapen   "to make cheaper"
quick → quicken   "to become faster"

OR, it forms a verb showing cause or becoming from a noun:

width → widen   "to become or make wider"

BRAIN TICKLERS
Set #78 Categorize -ION Words by Sound

Try sorting these -ion words by sound:

/kshən/, /shən/, or /zhən/.

act	→ action	inspect →	inspection
civilize	→ civilization	instruct →	instruction
complicate	→ complication	invade →	invasion
compose	→ composition	pollute →	pollution
confuse	→ confusion	predict →	prediction
decide	→ decision	profuse →	profusion
expose	→ exposition	reflect →	reflection
express	→ expression	regress →	regression
imprecise	→ imprecision		

(Answers are on page 226.)

We are us, ous, ious, eous

Delicious, *scrumptious*, and *nutritious*! How *generous* of you to share this treat with me without *animus*. Sounds delectable, right? But how do you know when to use which spelling of /əs/? We'll try to sort out this knotty-naughty homophonic problem.

And without animus, too!

- *-ous, ious,* and *-eous* all mean "characterized by or full of."
- *-us* is a singular Latin ending (the plural end is *-i*). It appears in words like:

Singular	Plural
alumnus	*alumni*
cactus	*cacti*
fungus	*fungi*
nucleus	*nuclei*
radius	*radii*

Its meaning puts it in a separate category from the other endings.

- Let's focus on *-ous, -ious* and *-eous* for a bit. When you attach them to a word, you can immediately hear the difference. Words like:

generous, callous, preposterous, and *joyous,* all with an /əs/ sound, sound different than *fallacious* /shəs/, *flirtatious* /shəs/, and *courteous* /ēəs/

- These words distinguish *-ous* and *-eous*, which make different sounds. So we're left trying to tell when to use *-cious* and when to use *-tious*, both of which sound like /shəs/. The suffix *-cious* is a lot more common, so that should help, for starters. Besides that, look at the base word and see if you can make connections between characteristics of the base words and which of the two suffixes it takes. The next Brain Tickler should help.

BRAIN TICKLERS
Set #79 Observe Patterns
in -IOUS and -EOUS Suffixes

For each group of words, write an obser-
vation about adding *-ious* or *-eous* to it.

-atious		**-eous**	
flirtation	flirtatious	spontaneity	spontaneous
vexation	vexatious	nauseate	nauseous
-acious		**-itious**	
capacity	capacious	nutrition	nutritious
audacity	audacious	ambition	ambitious
sagacity	sagacious		
mendacity	mendacious		
-nious		**-icious**	
harmony	harmonious	malice	malicious
ceremony	ceremonious	avarice	avaricious
felony	felonious	caprice	capricious
		office	officious
		suspicion	suspicious

(Answers are on page 227.)

Are you responsIBLE for choosing a suitABLE ending?

-able and *-ible* are a complicated pair.

MAY I INTRODUCE ABLE AND IBLE

Look at the following rules:

1. Most times that the ending is added to a whole word, you use *-able*, and when it is added to a base that cannot stand alone as a word, you add *-ible*.

Whole Word		**Root**	
depend	dependable	aud	audible
break	breakable	ed	edible

2. If the base word ends in silent *e*
   a. preceded by a soft *c* /s/ or *g* /j/, keep the *e* and add *-able*.

   manage   manageable   notice   noticeable

   b. without a soft *c* or *g*, drop the *e* and add *-able*.

   love   lovable   use   usable

3. If the *-ion* form of the word is
   a. spelled *-ation*, add *-able*.

admire	admiration	admirable
tolerate	toleration	tolerable
transport	transportation	transportable

   b. spelled without an *a*, add *-ible*, even though it IS a whole word.

contract	contraction	contractible
produce	production	producible

   c. spelled with *ss*, add *-ible* after the *ss*.

permit	permission	permissible
transmit	transmission	transmissible

There are some exceptions and additions to these rules (like *collapse*, which ends in silent *e*, but becomes *collapsible*), but these guidelines should stand you in pretty good stead.

BRAIN TICKLERS
Set #80 Add -ABLE and -IBLE Suffixes

Write the *-able* or *-ible* form of the following words and bases/roots:

admit	commend	read
apply	comprehend	-vis-
blame	contract	
change	-leg- /lĕj/	

(Answers are on page 228.)

Getting a hand/əl/ on /əl/

All spellings occur for a reason. But the /əl/ words have so many reasons for their different spellings that there's no simple way to categorize them. /əl/ can be spelled *el*, *le*, *al*, and occasionally *il* and *ol* (endings in *-ful* aren't included here). One important subset is *-acle*, *-icle*, and *-ical*.

BRAIN TICKLERS
Set #81 Categorize EL Words

Sometimes *el* spells the sound /əl/ at the end of a word, and sometimes it spells the sound /ĕl/. To help you remember that *el* can spell both these sounds, sort out the list of words into an /əl/ group and an /ĕl/ group.

compel	hotel	panel
excel	motel	weasel
gravel	nickel	

(Answers are on page 228.)

BRAIN TICKLERS
Set #82 /əl/ Word Search

Find as many /əl/ words as you can in the word find on page 219. (There are 59.) Group them by the spelling of the /əl/ sound: *el*, *le*, *al*, *il*, *ol*, *-acle*, *-icle*, or *-ical*. Words are horizontal, vertical, or diagonal, and may be forward or backward.

```
E L M P E N C I L L O E L A L O L I L A C L E E L
L E A E L C O C L I L V U L A L V E T L A C L E I
E L P E L A L I A E L W A F F L E E U O D D R A L
L E L E O M M C E R O L I L A C H E N R I U M M E
P R E T Z E L L E L O N K E M L I P N M M R R S S
L R E L U L D E D N D L L E M A C L E P P A R R F
H H E L Q R A S A N D A L A C L L E L E L E G G E
I S M M U P T T G G D L A T C L E E L E E R O C L
S E L C L E E L K E N N L I N I T I A L E A C C Z
T P P O N O L L E L D N A C N L O L L E D D U O O
O R I C M M A L R P L E L K E L E E L G N I J L O
R R I N B M B B N P P L L L E L B A F F C C U O B
I L E L A L M M E I L E L E F F B L F L E A M N M
C E L M O L Y I L R H M A C K E R E L E L L B E A
A V L L A C C A E S M A M M A L L T T L A O L L B
L I A O L R N L U S E L E G O B B L E L R R E S S
D N V B B G B B E L L A L A P B A S I L T L O Q E
D S I P E M M L S S K G G L A U B S E N N O D U L
F F T L U E Y L E I N N P L L B B V L E E D D I C
F E S B L E E S L G I E L U E L O L E L C I T R A
F E E L E S S U M N W A L O D H U L C L E L E R T
S E F L L E L T T A T L N E E D L E L E L E L E N
E S C O U N D R E L L I L O L E L A L I C L E L E
C E L A L I L O L U L A C L E I C E L C A R I M T
```

(Answers are on pages 228-229.)

And the rooster said, "ər, ər, ər, ər, ər!"

As you may recall from Chapter 1, some words that are spelled with an *-er* ending in American English are spelled in British English with *-re*, and these spellings are often listed in the dictionary. Here are some examples:

U.S. Spelling	British Spelling
caliber	calibre
center	centre
fiber	fibre
liter	litre
meter	metre
saber	sabre
somber	sombre

Another thing to consider in the United States is that words with an /ər/ sound at the end differ in the sound that precedes / r/ and in having two different spellings: *-er* and *-ure*. (One exception is *theater/theatre*, both of which are used in the United States.)

BRAIN TICKLERS
Set #83 Categorize Using Sight and Sound

Try sorting these by sound and sight. What categories do you find?

adventure	feature	picture
architecture	fracture	pleasure
closure	injure	poacher
composure	leisure	procedure
conjure	literature	sculpture
creature	measure	signature
culture	moisture	stretcher
disclosure	moocher	treasure
enclosure	overture	
exposure	pasture	

(Answers are on page 229.)

ANCE and ENCE: Please show AcceptANCE of their EquivalENCE

The endings *-nt*, *-nce*, and *-ncy* can all be preceded by either *e* or *a*. Some words take the ending *-ent*, and others take *-ant*. Some take *-ence*, whereas others take *-ance*. Some take *-ency*, and others take *-ancy*. Fortunately, words are consistent in taking *-e-* or *-a-* endings: *compete* takes *-ent*, and also takes *-ence* and *-ency*.

compete   competent   competence   competency

And words like *hesitate* that take *-ant*, also take *-ance* and *-ancy*.

| hesitate | hesitant | hesitance | hesitancy |

So once you know if a root word takes an *a* or an *e* in these endings, you're set. BUT . . . not every word can take all three suffixes. And sometimes the suffixes are attached to roots that cannot stand alone as words. The best thing to do is practice working with the groups.

BRAIN TICKLERS
Set #84 Add ENT/ANT, ENCE/ANCE, and ENCY/ANCY

For each word, give as many forms as it has for ent/ence/ency or ant/ance/ancy. If a form doesn't exist it has been *x*'d out in the chart for you.

Starter	ant/ent form	ance/ence form	ancy/ency form
accept			╳
allow	╳		
annoy	╳		
buoy			
coincide			╳
confide			╳
converse			

Starter	ant/ent form	ance/ence form	ancy/ency form
correspond			
depend			
differ			✕
dominate			
emerge			
equal			
excel			
exist			✕
expect			
grief	✕		✕
hesitate			
ignore			✕
import			✕
infant	✕	✕	
magnify			✕
obey			✕
persist			
recur			✕
rely			✕
revere			✕
signify			✕
vibrate			
violate			✕

(Answers are on page 230.)

BRAIN TICKLERS
Set #85 Provide Meanings for Five Rare Words Ending in ENT/ENCE

Some *ent/ence* words are pretty rare. For extra credit . . . over and above the call of duty . . . look up these five *ent/ence* words and note their meanings. Use the biggest dictionary you can find. (They're all in the *Oxford English Dictionary*.)

attingence   comburence   frugiferent
lutulence   regredience

(Answers are on page 231.)

BRAIN TICKLERS—THE ANSWERS

Set #72, page 205

g	resign, resignation
g	malign, malignant
n	condemn, condemnation
t	soft, soften, softly
a	economical, economically
b	debt, debit
b	doubt, dubious
d	grand, grandma
d	hand, handsome, handkerchief

Set #73, page 206

academician	consideration	invention
adoption	contortion	logistician
assertion	demonstration	magician
association	discrimination	musician
attraction	electrician	pediatrician
circulation	exception	politician
clinician	inhibition	reflection
completion	inspection	selection
composition	instruction	statistician

Set #74, page 208

centrality	short *a*	/ă/
economics	short *o*	/ŏ/
formality	short *a*	/ă/
metallic	short *a*	/ă/
relativity	short *i*	/ĭ/

Set #75, page 209

bilious	short *i*	/ĭ/
conic	short *o*	/ŏ/
criminal	short *i*	/ĭ/
diabetic	short *e*	/ĕ/
divinity	short *i*	/ĭ/
mimic	short *i*	/ĭ/
sanity	short *a*	/ă/
serenity	short *e*	/ĕ/
static	short *a*	/ă/
tonic	short *o*	/ŏ/
volcanic	short *a*	/ă/

Set #76, page 210

admiration	long *i* /ī/ goes to /ə/
coincident	long *i* /ī/ goes to /ə/
definition	long *i* /ī/ goes to /ə/
president	long *i* /ī/ goes to /ə/
resident	long *i* /ī/ goes to /ə/

Possible responses: *perspire → perspiration   inspire → inspiration*

Set #77, page 212

Words ending in *de* drop the *de* and add *-sion*.			
decide	decision	erode	erosion
evade	evasion	conclude	conclusion

Words ending in *ose* drop the *e* and add an *i* before *-tion*			
compose	composition	suppose	supposition
expose	exposition	transpose	transposition

Words ending in *ize* drop the *e* and add an *a* before *-tion*			
civilize	civilization	specialize	specialization
realize	realization	capitalize	capitalization

Words ending in *x* and *nt* add *a* before *-tion*.			
relax	relaxation	document	documentation
tax	taxation	indent	indentation
vex	vexation	lament	lamentation
fix	fixation	plant	plantation

Words ending in *ss* add *-ion*.			
express	expression	possess	possession
regress	regression	impress	impression

Words ending in *ate, ise, use,* and *ute* drop the *e* and add *-ion*.			
agitate	agitation	televise	television
complicate	complication	profuse	profusion
concentrate	concentration	constitute	constitution
educate	education	contribute	contribution
confuse	confusion	pollute	pollution
imprecise	imprecision	substitute	substitution

Words ending in *ct* add *-ion*.			
act	action	predict	prediction
reflect	reflection	instruct	instruction

These visual groups can help you predict spelling, but there are exceptions.

Set #78, page 213

/kshən/			
act	action	predict	prediction
inspect	inspection	reflect	reflection
instruct	instruction		

/shən/			
civilize	civilization	express	expression
complicate	complication	pollute	pollution
compose	composition	regress	regression
expose	exposition		

/zhən/			
confuse	confusion	invade	invasion
decide	decision	profuse	profusion
imprecise	imprecision		

Set #79, page 215

Answers may vary. Possible responses:

-atious Words that have an *-ation* form take *-atious*.			
flirtation	flirtatious	vexation	vexatious

-acious Words that have an *-acity* form take *-acious*.			
capacity	capacious	sagacity	sagacious
audacity	audacious	mendacity	mendacious

-nious Words that have an *-ony* form take *-nious*.			
harmony	harmonious	felony	felonious
ceremony	ceremonious		

-eous Words with an *e* after the last consonant in the root take *e*.			
spontaneity	spontaneous	nauseate	nauseous

-itious Words with an *-ition* form take *-itious*.			
nutrition	nutritious	ambition	ambitious

-icious Words with an *-ic(e)* take *-icious*.			
malice	malicious	office	officious
avarice	avaricious	suspicion	suspicious
caprice	capricious		

Set #80, page 217

admit	admissible	comprehend	comprehensible
apply	applicable	contract	contractible
blame	blamable	leg- /lĕj/	legible
change	changeable	read	readable
commend	commendable	vis-	visible

Set #81, page 218

/ĕl/		/əl/	
compel	hotel	gravel	panel
excel	motel	nickel	weasel

Set #82, page 218

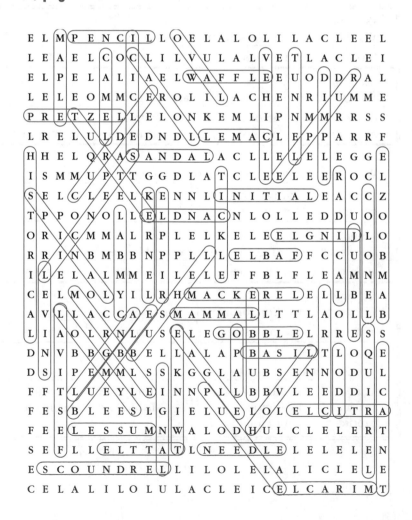

LE

bamboozle	fable	puddle
bubble	gobble	ripple
bumble	jingle	rumple
camel	jumble	tattle
candle	maple	tickle
curdle	marble	turtle
dimple	needle	twinkle
eagle	pretzel	waffle

ACLE

miracle	tentacle

ICLE

article	icicle	vehicle

ICAL

historical	radical

AL

central	mammal	signal
cymbal	opal	spinal
festival	oval	
initial	sandal	

EL

angel	hovel	scoundrel
bushel	kernel	snivel
camel	mackerel	squirrel
colonel	mussel	tunnel

OL

carol	idol	symbol

IL

basil	pencil	stencil

Set #83, page 221

Two Syllables		
/chər/		
creature	moisture	poacher
culture	moocher	sculpture
feature	pasture	stretcher
fracture	picture	
/zhər/		
closure	measure	treasure
leisure	pleasure	
/jər/		
conjure	injure	

Three or More Syllables		
/chər/ adventure architecture	literature overture	signature
/zhər/ composure disclosure	enclosure	exposure
/jər/ procedure		

Set #84, page 222

	ant/ent form	ance/ence form	ancy/ency form
accept	acceptant	acceptance	
allow		allowance	
annoy		annoyance	
buoy	buoyant	buoyance	buoyancy
coincide	coincident	coincidence	
confide	confident	confidence	
converse	conversant	conversance	conversancy
correspond	correspondent	correspondence	correspondency
depend	dependent	dependence	dependency
differ	different	difference	
dominate	dominant	dominance	dominancy
emerge	emergent	emergence	emergency
equal	equivalent	equivalence	equivalency
excel	excellent	excellence	excellency
exist	existent	existence	
expect	expectant	expectance	expectancy
grief		grievance	
hesitate	hesitant	hesitance	hesitancy
ignore	ignorant	ignorance	
import	important	importance	
infant			infancy

magnify	magnificent	magnificence	
obey	obedient	obedience	
persist	persistent	persistence	persistency
recur	recurrent	recurrence	
rely	reliant	reliance	
revere	reverent	reverence	
signify	significant	significance	
vibrate	vibrant	vibrance	vibrancy
violate	violent	violence	

Set #85, page 224

attingence: influence
comburence: ability to cause combustion, that is, start a fire
frugiferent: bearing fruit
lutulence: muddiness
regredience: return

CHAPTER NINE

Confusing Words

HOMOGRAPHS, HOMOPHONES, AND HOMONYMS

Present a present and record a record

Homophones, as we've mentioned, are groups of (usually two) words that sound the same but are spelled differently. Homographs are groups of (usually two) words that are spelled the same way but have different meanings. There are several kinds of homographs.

Related verbs and nouns (like record´ and re´cord) with the same spelling but different pronunciations, are not technically homographs according to some because they have the same etymological root, but we're going to include them here because they can present a spelling challenge: you have to remember that even though they sound different, they're spelled the same.

Other related parts of speech can be homographs AND homophones at the same time. When one, for example, has a comparative ending -er and the other has the noun suffix -er, you get homographs like:

stranger (the person you don't know) and *stranger* (more strange)

cooler (the place you keep things so they don't get warm) and *cooler* (more cool).

BRAIN TICKLERS
Set #86 Find Homographs That Aren't Homophones

For each word in the list below, look in the dictionary to find definitions for two homographs that are NOT homophones. Record the definitions.

1. bass   3. gill   5. real

2. bow   4. lead

(Answers are on page 240.)

BRAIN TICKLERS
Set #87 Use Homographs to Complete a Crossword Puzzle

Use the clues to help you discover the homographs that will complete the crossword puzzle.

DOWN

1. Several female deer, or the third person singular of a verb meaning "to carry out"

3. Very small, or a duration of time equal to 60 seconds

4. The quality of not being dead, or a verb meaning "to reside in a place"

6. A kind of fish with both eyes on one side of its head, or to thrash about helplessly and without effect

7. Creating a small, bright sound as by hitting a crystal with a pencil, or coloring something slightly

8. Hitting a golf ball a short distance, or the act of placing something in a spot

9. Moving air, or the act of wrapping up something into a ball

ACROSS

2. To start up again, or an organized list of one's activities and employment

5. To strike with sharp blows, or a display of food from which guests may serve themselves

9. Wrapped up string into a ball, or an injury that breaks the skin

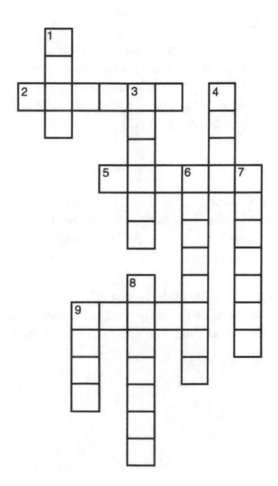

(Answers are on page 240.)

What's /sôs/ for the goose may be /sŏs/ for the gander

Different people may have different homophones. Why? Because homophones depend on pronunciation, and people with different dialects pronounce words differently. What's a homophone for you may not be a homophone for your best friend.

Hum oh funs

There are several kinds of homophones:

- Single words that come from the same origin, but evolved differently (complacent, complaisant).
- Single words that have different origins (creak, creek).
- A single word that sounds identical to a word from another language (curd, kurd).

Homonyms

When a pair of homographs are also homophones, we call them *homonyms*. Got that? They're word pairs that are spelled the same AND pronounced the same. Examples are:

- cricket (the game and the insect)
- can (the container and the verb that means "to be able")
- fine (the penalty and the adjective meaning "good")

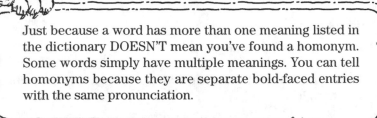

Just because a word has more than one meaning listed in the dictionary DOESN'T mean you've found a homonym. Some words simply have multiple meanings. You can tell homonyms because they are separate bold-faced entries with the same pronunciation.

BRAIN TICKLERS
Set #88 Find Homophones and Homonyms

1. Write a homophone for each word listed.

brews	freeze	pores
brows	grays	tax
daze	hose	tease
doze	nose	wax
flew		

2. How many sets of homonyms can you list in five minutes? Time yourself and see. (No fair using the homophones from #1.)

(Answers are on page 241.)

BRAIN TICKLERS—THE ANSWERS

Set #86, page 235

Possible responses include the following:

1. **bass:** a freshwater fish; a man with a low singing voice; a fibrous plant product

2. **bow:** the front of a ship; to bend one's body in recognition of applause; a rod strung with horsehair and used for playing a string instrument such as a violin

3. **gill:** a fish's respiratory organ; a unit of liquid measure equal to 1/2 cup

4. **lead:** to guide; a soft metal

5. **real:** actually the case; a Portuguese and Brazilian monetary unit

Set #87, page 236

Set #88, page 239

1. brews/bruise   hose/hoes
   brows/browse   nose/knows/no's
   daze/days   pores/pours
   doze/doughs   tax/tacks
   flew/flue   tease/teas
   freeze/frieze/frees wax/whacks
   grays/graze

2. Possible responses:
   bank: the earth beside a river; a monetary institution
   bark: the sound a dog makes; the covering on a tree trunk
   barrow: short for wheelbarrow; a burial mound or hill
   bellows: yells loudly; a tool for providing oxygen to a fire
   bound: tied up; headed towards
   can: a metal container; capable of
   champ: to chew; the champion
   cricket: a sport; an insect resembling a grasshopper
   fare: amount required for a bus/subway/taxi ride; food
   fine: a penalty; good
   firm: unyielding; a company
   fit: a seizure; in good shape, healthy
   flat: an apartment; a level
   hail: to greet; hard, round precipitation called "hailstones"
   hamper: to get in the way of; a container, especially for dirty laundry
   last: a shoemaker's tool; the final one
   leaves: goes away; the things that fall off trees in autumn
   mews: a back street; the noise a cat makes
   mine: a deep pit, dug to allow removal of gems and minerals from the earth; something that belongs to me
   pants: breathes heavily to reduce internal body temperature; slacks
   plane: a two-dimensional surface; a type of tree
   quarry: something that's being hunted; a place where stones are mined
   rest: a nap; what's left over
   rose: a flower; got up
   row: an argument; to use an oar or set of oars to propel a boat
   stable: steady; a place to keep horses

CHAPTER TEN

Greek and Latin Base Words

BASE WORD FAMILIES

In Chapter 7 we talked about prefixes with Greek and Latin origins, as well as Latin plurals. Since many important base words also come to us from Greek and Latin and form the foundation of some hefty word families, we're going to take some time to focus on them here. The important point from a spelling perspective is that these word families all have a family resemblance, kind of like everyone in a family having curly hair or freckles—some feature that helps you identify that they go together. For the

most part, once you know the spelling of a base, there is not a lot of variation. If you can spell *metr/meter*, the Greek root meaning "measure," you can spell it in *symmetry*, *diameter*, *metric*, *geometry*, *thermometer*, and so on. Familiarity with these widely used roots will improve your spelling.

BRAIN TICKLERS
Set #89 Find English Words
with Given Greek and Latin Roots

Just to get you started . . . take a look at these root words and their meanings. Write as many English words as you can that have each root word. You can use a dictionary if you wish. Remember that you can have the root word appear at the beginning, middle, or end of an English word, and you can add prefixes, suffixes, or both to it.

Greek Root	Meaning	Example in English
aster/astr	star	astronaut
auto	self	automatic
chron	time	chronic
graph	writing	paragraph
Latin Root	**Meaning**	**Example in English**
scrib/script	to write	scribe
son	sound	sonic
verb	word	verbal
voc/vok	to call/voice	vocal chords

(Answers are on page 258.)

Sound familiar?

It's easier to remember a group of interconnected words than just a random list of roots. So let's look at some logically connected groups of root words. First let's focus on words having to do with sound.

Sound			
Root Word	**Meaning**	**Language of Origin**	**Example**
dic/dict	speak	Latin	dictate
phe/phem	speak	Greek	euphemism
gloss/glott/glot	tongue/language	Greek	polyglot
lingu	language/tongue	Latin	linguistic
aud	hear	Latin	audible
ora	speech/mouth	Latin	oracle
phon	sound	Greek	phonograph

BRAIN TICKLERS
Set #90 Find English Words with Given Roots

How many English words can you discover that contain at least one of the root words in the Sound chart: dic/dict, phe/phem, gloss/glott/glot, lingu, aud, ora, and phon.

(Answers are on page 259.)

Vision revision

Many English words having to do with looking, seeing, the eye, and tools used with the eye have Greek and Latin roots.

Sight			
Root Word	**Meaning**	**Language of Origin**	**Example**
luc	light	Latin	lucid
ocul	eye	Latin	ocular
ops/opt/op	sight; eye	Greek	optical
photo/phos	light	Greek	photograph
scope	instrument for viewing	Greek	microscope
spect	look	Latin	prospect
vid/vis	to see	Latin	video

BRAIN TICKLERS
Set #91 Define Words from Known Roots

This time, tell the meaning of each word made from one of the roots in the sight chart.

photograph   phosphorescent
telescope   elucidate
inspect   monocle
invisible   ophthalmologist

Look up the word in a dictionary if you need to.

(Answers are on page 259.)

To life!

Here is a group of words related to life.

Life			
Root Word	**Meaning**	**Language of Origin**	**Example**
anim	spirit/life	Latin	animated
dendr/dender	tree	Greek	dendrology
spir	to breathe	Latin	perspire
vit/viv	life	Latin	vital
zoo	animal	Greek	zoo

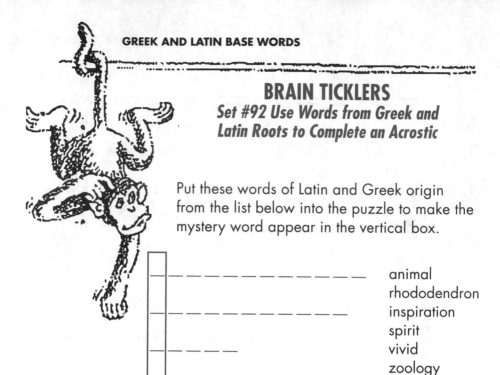

BRAIN TICKLERS
Set #92 Use Words from Greek and Latin Roots to Complete an Acrostic

Put these words of Latin and Greek origin from the list below into the puzzle to make the mystery word appear in the vertical box.

animal
rhododendron
inspiration
spirit
vivid
zoology

(Answers are on page 260.)

The law of the land

Just as our legal system and our system of government have their origins in Greece and Rome, so many of our words having to do with right and justice (the judicial branch) and governing (the executive branch) come from these two civilizations.

Hey! Watch your step!

Right/Justice

Root Word	Meaning	Language of Origin	Example
bon/ben	good	Latin	bonus
crit/cris	judge	Greek	critical
dox	opinion	Greek	paradox
eth	moral	Greek	ethos
jud	judge	Latin	judge
mal	bad	Latin	malfunction
nom	law	Greek	Deuteronomy
ortho	correct/straight	Greek	orthopedics
soph	wise	Greek	sophisticated
val	strong/worth	Latin	valuable

Governing

Root Word	Meaning	Language of Origin	Example
arch	rule/govern	Greek	matriarch
cracy	rule/government	Greek	autocracy
dem	people	Greek	epidemic
ethn	nation	Greek	ethnicity
pol/polis	city, state	Greek	politics

BRAIN TICKLERS
Set #93 Use Words Related to
Law to Complete a Crossword Puzzle

Read each clue and write the word containing one of the "Law of the Land" roots that fits into the crossword puzzle. Notice which spelling is used for the roots that have alternate forms. The roots are: *bon/ben, crit/cirs, dox, eth, jud, mal, nom, ortho soph, val, arch, cracy, dem, ethn,* and *pol/polis.*

DOWN

1. Accepting an established doctrine

4. To evaluate

5. The absence of a ruler

6. Wrongdoing by someone who holds public office

7. Not legally valid

8. Having to do with a major city

ACROSS

2. Principles of moral value

3. Having to do with courts of law

9. Working for the good of

10. Reasoning that appears wise, but isn't

11. Rule by the people

12. Relating to racial and cultural heritage

13. Rule of a single person by him/herself

(Answers are on page 260.)

Miscellaneous but not extraneous

Here are three more categories—size, love, and study—and a challenge to go with them.

Size		
Root Word	Meaning	Language of Origin
magna	large	Latin
mega/megalo	large	Greek
micro	small	Greek

Love		
Root Word	Meaning	Language of Origin
ama/ami	love	Latin
philo	love	Greek

Study		
Root Word	Meaning	Language of Origin
doc/doct	teach	Latin
gno/gnos	know	Greek
logo	word/reason	Greek
sci	know	Latin
ver	truth	Latin

BRAIN TICKLERS
Set #94 Find Words That Contain Given Greek and Latin Roots

If you can find one word that contains each root word from the charts, you're floating; two, and you're in orbit; three or more, and you're on the astral plane.

(Answers are on page 261.)

BRAIN TICKLERS
Set #95 Write a Composition Containing Words with Greek and Latin Roots

Now it's time to review what you've learned. Write a composition in which you use at least ten words, each having a different Greek or Latin root used in this chapter. You can write a short story, a news story, a diary entry, or any other kind of piece that strikes your fancy. Try to choose your topic carefully to make your work easier.

(Answers are on page 262.)

BRAIN TICKLERS
Set #96 Combine Prefixes and Roots

The final challenge . . . Can you take some of the prefixes from Chapter 7 and combine them with the roots here to make new words? Use clues to help you. Combine Greek prefixes with Greek roots and Latin prefixes with Latin roots. Use a dictionary to help you if you need to.

Greek Prefixes	Clues: Make Words That Mean:
a- (*an-*) without, not	"not knowing" "without leadership"
anti- against, opposite	"against the law" "opposition"
auto- self	"rule by a single person"
dia- through, together	"to talk together"
eu- good, pleasant	"a pleasant way of speaking about an unpleasant topic"
hyper- extra, over, excessive, beyond	"overcritical"
micro- very small	"an instrument that enlarges a small sound"
para- beside, similar to, beyond	"beyond opinion"
peri- about, around	"an instrument that allows one to look around corners"
pseudo- false, pretended, not real	"with a false appearance of refinement

Latin Prefixes	Clues: Make Words That Mean:
bi- two	"having two lenses" "for both eyes"
circum- around, on all sides	"to look around" "prudent"
de- reversal, removal, away, from, off, down	"to reduce the value of"
multi- many	"able to speak many languages"
pre- before	"to evaluate before sufficient evidence is available"
re- again, back, backward	"to look at again in order to correct" "to make move again" "to make live again"
trans- across, beyond	"letting light shine through" "to breathe out"

(Answers are on page 263.)

BRAIN TICKLERS—THE ANSWERS

Set #89, page 246

Possible responses:

Greek	
aster/astr	asterisk asteroid astral astrocyte astrodome astrodynamics astrogate astrology astrometry astronautics astronavigation astronomer astronomical astronomy astrophotography astrophysics astrosphere disaster
auto	autobiographer autobiography autochrome autochthon autoclave autocrat autograph autoharp autohypnosis automat automobile autonomy autopsy photoautotroph semiautobiographical semiautomatic
chron	anachronism chronicle chronograph chronology chronometer dendrochronology synchronize
graph	autobiography autograph bibliography biography calligraphy grapheme graphic graphite phonograph photograph telegraph

Latin	
scrib/script	ascribe circumscribe describe description inscribe inscription manuscript nondescript prescribe prescription scribble script scripture subscribe transcribe transcript
son	consonant diapason dissonance resonance sonata sonnet sonogram sonorous
verb	adverb nonverbal proverb reverb verbal verbalize verbatim verbiage verbose
voc/vok	advocate equivocate evoke invocation invoice irrevocable provoke provocateur revoke subvocalize vocabulary vocal vocalist vocation vociferous .

Set #90, page 248

aud	audience, audio, audition, auditorium, auditory, inaudible
dic/dict	benediction, contradict, contradiction, dictator, diction dictionary, edict, indict, malediction
gloss/glott/glot	epiglottis, glottal, gloss, glossary, glossolalia, polyglot
lingu	bilingual, lingo, linguine(!), linguist
ora	oracle, oral, oration, oratorio
phe/phem	blaspheme, prophet
phon	aphonic, cacophony, euphony, megaphone, microphone, orthophonic, phonics, polyphony, symphony, telephone

Set #91, page 249

photograph: a print made on light-sensitive paper
telescope: an instrument to see things that are far away
inspect: to look at closely
invisible: not able to be seen
phosphorescent: permitting emission of light after exposure to radiation
elucidate: to bring to light; to make plain
monocle: a single lens used to improve vision
ophthalmologist: a physician specializing in the function and diseases of the eye

Set #92, page 250

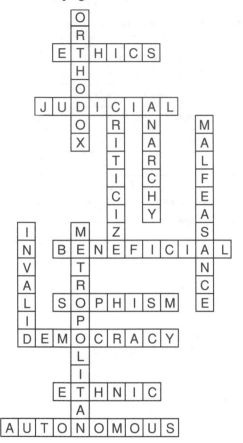

Set #93, page 252

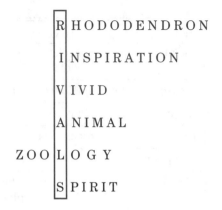

R HODODENDRON

I NSPIRATION

V IVID

A NIMAL

ZOO L OGY

S PIRIT

The words spell *rivals*, which is the mystery word. Rivals, which comes from Latin, originally meant "those who share a stream" and now means competitors.

While at the zoo, the dendrologist began to perspire when the vital life-form became a little too animated.

Set #94, page 255

Size	
magna	magnanimous magnate magnification magnificent magnify magniloquent magnitude
mega/megalo	megabucks megabyte megahertz megalith megalomaniac megalopolis megaphone megavitamin
micro	microbe microbiology microchip microeconomics microelectronics micromanage microphone
Love	
ama/ami	amateur amiable amicable amigo amity
philo	Anglophile bibliophile hemophilia Philadelphia philanthropy philately philodendron philology philosophy
Study	
doc/doct	docile doctor doctorate doctrine docudrama documentary indoctrinate
gno/gnos	agnostic diagnosis gnosticism prognosticate
logo	analogy archaeology catalogue dialogue eulogy genealogy geology logic monologue prologue syllogism
sci	omniscient prescience science scientific scientist
ver	veracious veracity veridical verdict verification verify verisimilitude veritable verity

Set #95, page 255

Possible response: a poem

Once there was an <u>astronaut</u>, who also was a <u>polyglot</u>.

He went on many <u>astral</u> trips in spaceships that used <u>microchips.</u>

He wasn't one to cry or mope. He <u>verified</u> sightings through his <u>telescope</u>.

One day, alas, his spaceship crashed; his fine equipment all was trashed.

He went out to <u>inspect</u> the mess, and think and probe and <u>judge</u> and guess

and <u>prospect</u> for some things of worth, so he could travel back to Earth.

<u>Prognosticating</u> by the moon, he hoped that he could get back soon.

Employing <u>scientific</u> means, he built a worthy craft, it seems.

For since arriving back today, he's left to vacation in Paraguay.

But soon he'll be back out in space, exploring some new distant place.

Set #96, page 256

Greek	
"not knowing"	agnostic
"without leadership"	anarchy
"against the law" "opposition"	antinomy
"rule by a single person"	autocracy
"to talk together"	dialogue
"a pleasant way of speaking about an unpleasant topic"	euphemism
"overcritical"	hypercritical
"an instrument that enlarges a small sound"	microphone
"beyond opinion"	paradox
"an instrument that allows one to look around corners"	periscope
"with a false appearance of refinement"	pseudo-sophisticated

Latin	
"having two lenses" "for both eyes"	binoculars
"to look around" "prudent"	circumspect
"to reduce the value of"	devalue

"able to speak many languages"	multilingual
"to evaluate before sufficient evidence is available"	prejudge
"to look at again in order to correct"	revision
"to make move again"	reanimate
"to make live again"	revive
"letting light shine through"	translucent
"to breathe out"	transpire

Predictable Spelling Changes

ACCOMMODATION:
NOW YOU SEE IT, NOW YOU DON'T

In Chapter 8 we talked about alternations—changes in sound
that occur even though spelling stays the same. Now we're going
to discuss changes in spelling that come about mainly to make
words easier to pronounce. When we add affixes to roots, sometimes the result is kind of hard to say. We **accommodate** these
situations with little shifts in spelling that help us get our
tongues around the words.

Look at these suffix additions and try saying the results without and with the accommodation. Which works best, do you
think?

Root + Suffix	Result without Accommodation	Pronunciation	Result with Accommodation
erode + sion	erodsion	/ĭr-ōd′shən/	erosion
comprehend + sion	comprehendsion	/kŏm-prĭ-hĕnd′shən/	comprehension
introduce + tion	introducetion	/ĭn-trə-do͞os′shən/	introduction
magic + ian	magician	/mă-jĭk′shən/	magician

WOW!

Better, right?

e r o s i o n

Remember this? Changes at the syllable juncture

Remember how we dealt with spelling changes needing to match sound changes when we added /ən/? Then we were differentiating /ən/ endings. Now we're going to focus on the spelling changes that happen when these suffixes are added.

D and DE changes	**erode** *de* spells /d/	→	**erosion** *s(i)* spells /zh/
	comprehend *d* spells /d/	→	**comprehension** *s(i)* spells /sh/
CE changes	**introduce** *ce* spells /s/	→	**introduction** *c* spells /k/
C changes	**magic** *c* spells /k/	→	**magician** *c(i)* spells /sh/

BRAIN TICKLERS
Set #97 Add -ION and -IAN Suffixes and Categorize Results

Write the *-ion* or *-ian* form of each word given below. Group the resulting words into the groups represented in the chart above:

D → S   DE → S   CE → C   C → CI

collide	extend	music	produce
decide	include	persuade	reduce
delude	invade	politic	statistic
explode	mathematics		

(Answers are on page 279.)

What's happening to my vowels?

Sometimes adding a suffix changes more than just the syllable juncture. Yes, back in the middle of the word, things can change, too. Remember how adding a suffix can change pronunciation? We talked about these alternations in Chapter 8. Often, these changes were either from or to a schwa sound, and since schwa can be spelled with virtually any vowel letter, the spelling didn't change.

Now we're getting to more sophisticated changes: Sometimes the sound AND the spelling change. Remember the word *morpheme*? It's the smallest unit of language that has meaning and cannot be subdivided. However, a single morpheme can have more than one appearance or shape. When you have more than one visual/sound form of a morpheme, the multiple forms are called **allomorphs**. Here are two examples:

vain in *vain* and **van** in *vanity* are the same morpheme. When you add the suffix *-ity* the *ai* becomes an *a*, and the vowel sound changes from long to short. In adding the suffix *-ity* to a word like *insane*, dropping the *e* is enough to signal the change from a long to a short vowel sound. No other spelling change is needed.

sume in *consume* and **sump** in *consumption* are also the same morpheme. When you add the suffix *-tion* the long *u* sound marked by the final *e* changes to a short sound *u* shown visually by a double consonant—again, a change from long to short. Notice that in both cases, the accented syllable remains the same.

Some allomorphs have a long version and a schwa version for when the accentuation changes syllables, and often the spelling changes as well. So we get:

ex-plain′ → ex-pla na′tion **plain** → **plan** and the accent moves to the following syllable
ex-claim′ → ex-cla ma′tion **claim** → **clam** and the accent moves to the following syllable

Notice how the initial vowel in the digraph stays the same—the vowel with which the sound is named—and the second vowel is dropped.

BRAIN TICKLERS
Set #98 Predict Vowel Changes
When Adding Suffixes

Given the previous examples, predict the vowel change for each bold syllable when adding the suffix indicated. Then write the word with the suffix. Use a dictionary if you need to.

re**ceive** + tion
per**ceive** + tion
de**ceive** + tion
state + ic
tone + ic

bile + ious
grain + ular
mime + ic
flame + able

(Answers are on page 279.)

ASSIMILATION INVESTIGATION— MEET THE CHAMELEONS

And I thought I knew a thing or two about assimilation!

Now we're going to wind up our exploration of spelling with the most changeable of all morphemes: a set of prefixes that change their final consonant in order to better fit with the root or base word they attach to. Just like a chameleon that changes its color to match its surroundings, these guys change their shape to better fit in with whatever follows—to smooth out the syllable juncture, as it were. This can make them tricky to recognize, because they look one way one time, and a different way the next time— these prefixes have more allomorphs than you can shake a stick at. So let's start off by meeting them.

The basic six

Here they are:

Prefix	Meaning(s)
ad-	to, toward
com-	with
in-	not, into
ob-	against, toward
sub-	under
syn-	together, with

BRAIN TICKLERS
Set #99 Define Words Formed with Assimilating Prefixes

Write the meaning of each word. (Note: you're going to find some unusual words here, because we're going to use only bases that are words.) Use a dictionary if you need to. Notice how the affix joins onto the word.

ad-	adjoin	administer
com-	commingle	compromise
in-	incapable	insufficient
ob-	oblong	obnoxious
sub-	submarine	subsoil
syn-	synoptic	synchronic

(Answers are on page 279.)

Ad- it up

There are TEN allomorphs for *ad-* (including *ad-* itself). The prefix *ad-* turns to *a-* before *sc, sp, st,* and *gn.* Otherwise, *ad-*'s consonant matches the consonant it precedes either by doubling it or making a sound easy to pronounce.

Allomorph	Sample Word
ac-	accompany acquaintance
ad-	adjoin
af-	affirm
ag-	aggrieve
al-	allot
an-	annotate
ap-	appetite
ar-	arrest
as-	assort
at-	attune

How do you know if the word part you're looking at is an allomorph of *ad-* or some other morpheme? Look at the etymology in the dictionary entry. For example, if you look up *accompany* and look at the etymology all the way back to the origins of the word, it will say something like *ad-* + *compaignon.* That *ad-* in the etymology tells you that *ac-* is an allomorph of *ad-.*

Did you notice how many doubled consonants there are at the syllable juncture of the prefix and the root or base word, like in *accompany*? That's one of the signs of an assimilated prefix.

BRAIN TICKLERS
Set #100 Find Words for Allomorphs of AD-

Find one example of a word for each allomorph of *ad-*. It can be attached to a base word or a root word.

(Answers are on page 280.)

In- at the beginning

There are five allomorphs of *in-*.

Allomorph of *in*	Sample Word
i- (before *g*)	ignominy
il- (before *l*)	illegal
im- (before *b, m, p*)	immortal
in- (the rest of the time)	incapable
ir- (before *r*)	irrational

BRAIN TICKLERS
Set #101 Find Words for Allomorphs of IN-

Find two examples of words for each allomorph of *in-*. They can be attached to a base word or a root word. How many of the ten have a doubled consonant at the syllable juncture between the prefix and the root or base word?

(Answers are on page 280.)

Don't let *com-* con you

The prefix *com-* has four allomorphs.

Allomorphs of *com-*	Sample Word
it's *com-* (before *b*, *m*, and *p)*	combine complain commerce
it's *co-* (before *h*, *g*, *gn*, and usually before vowels)	cogent coherent cognition
it's *cor-* (before *r*, it's *col* before *l)*	collaborate corroborate
it's *con-* (before other consonants)	conjecture

BRAIN TICKLERS
Set #102 Find Words for
Allomorphs of COM-

Find a word for each allomorph of *com-*
and use them to write a poem.

(Answers are on page 280.)

Toward an understanding of *ob-*

The prefix *ob-* has five allomorphs.

Allomorphs of *ob-*	Sample Words
o- before *m*	omit
oc- before *c*	occur
of- before *f*	offend
op- before *p*	oppose
ob- the rest of the time	observe

Sub-pose we learn about *sub-*

The pefix *sub-* is not just for submarines! Take a look at its eight allomorphs:.

Allomorphs of *sub-*	Sample Words
suf- before *f*	suffix
sug- before *g*	suggest
sum- before *m*	summon
sup- before *p*	suppose
sur- before *r*	surreptitious
sus- sometimes before *c*, *p*, *t*	suspect
sub- before all else	submarine

BRAIN TICKLERS
Set #103 Find a Word with a Prefix to Match Each Clue

Find a *sub* or *ob* word to match each clue. A hint tells you which allomorph to use for each.

1. Under the basement *(sub)*
2. No longer in use *(ob)*
3. Brief and clear *(suc)*
4. To enslave *(op)*
5. To maintain *(sus)*
6. To make something available *(sup)*

(Answers are on page 280.)

Syn- is with us

Last one. Are you ready for *sym-* and its four allomorphs?

Allomorphs of *sym-*	Sample Words
sym- before *b, m, p*	symbiotic, symmetrical, sympathy
syl- before *l*	syllable
sy- before *s* and *z*	system, syzygy
syn- elsewhere	syntax

BRAIN TICKLERS
Set #104 Match Words and Clues

Match the words with the definitions.

Words
1. syllogism
2. symphony
3. synchronize
4. syncretism
5. syndrome
6. syzygy

Definitions
a. set of signs that indicates a disease
b. combining of different belief systems
c. to happen in unison
d. long sonata for orchestra
e. point at which a celestial body is in conjunction with the sun
f. reasoning from the general to the specific

And on that excellent spelling bee word—*syzygy*—we end.

(Answers are on page 280.)

BRAIN TICKLERS—THE ANSWERS

Set #97, page 268

D → S	extension		
DE → S	collision	explosion	persuasion
	decision	inclusion	
	delusion	invasion	
CE → C	production	reduction	
C → CI	mathematician	politician	
	musician	statistician	

Set #98, page 270

re**ceive** + tion	drop *ive*, add *p*	reception
per**ceive** + tion	drop *ive*, add *p*	preception
de**ceive** + tion	drop *ive*, add *p*	deception
state + ic	drop *e*	static
tone + ic	drop *e*	tonic
bile + ious	drop *e*	bilious
grain + ular	drop *i*	granular
mime + ic	drop *e*	mimic
flame + able	drop *e*	flammable

Set #99, page 272

adjoin	to be next to
administer	to direct
commingle	to mingle with
compromise	to settle differences with
incapable	not capable
insufficient	not sufficient
oblong	elongated in one direction
obnoxious	very annoying
submarine	a ship that can operate beneath the water
subsoil	the layer of earth under the topsoil
synoptic	presenting a report from the same point of view
synchronic	occurring at the same time

Set #100, page 274

Possible responses:

a-	ascend	**ag-**	aggravate	**ar-**	arrange
ac-	accustom, acquire	**al-**	allocate	**as-**	assimilate
ad-	admire	**an-**	announce	**at-**	attend
af	affix	**ap-**	appall		

Set #101, page 275

Possible responses:

i-	ignore, ignoble		**in-**	inaccurate, inappropriate
il-	illegible, illuminate		**ir-**	irresponsible, irregular
im-	immaterial, immature			

Six have a doubled consonant.

Set #102, page 276

Possible responses:

co-	coexist	**com-**	compare
col-	collect	**con-**	construct, conclude (one extra!)
cor-	correct		

How can I <u>construct</u> a poem that makes sense
When I'm feeling rather dense?
How many allomorphs must I <u>collect</u>?
It's hard to get them all <u>correct</u>.
Why should so many forms <u>coexist</u>?
I have to keep adding to my list.
When each prefix I <u>compare,</u>
I just <u>conclude</u> it isn't fair.

Set #103, page 277

1. subbasement
2. obsolete
3. succinct
4. oppress
5. sustain
6. supply

Set #104, page 278

1. f
2. d
3. c
4. b
5. a
6. e

INDEX

Pages in boldface indicate where terms are defined.

Really. This isn't going to hurt at all . . .

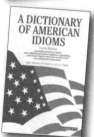

Get access to your exclusive PAINLESS SPELLING mobile app

Just visit *www.BarronsBooks.com/painless.html*

To face the ultimate Spelling and Arcade Action Game Challenge!

A s

for every

Painl

www.bar
There y
how to
contair
knowled
arcad